# Trinny and Susannah

## What you wear can change your life

# Trinny and Susannah

## What you wear can change your life

**Trinny Woodall and
Susannah Constantine**

Photography by Robin Matthews

WEIDENFELD & NICOLSON

# To Zak, Joe, Esme, Cece and Lyla

First published in Great Britain in 2004
by Weidenfeld & Nicolson

By arrangement with the BBC
The BBC logo is a trade mark of the British Broadcasting Corporation
and is used under licence.
BBC logo © BBC 1996
What Not to Wear logo © BBC 2002

Hair by Richard Ward Hair & Beauty, London
Make-up by Charlotte Ribeyro
Styling by Zoe Lem and Hayley Parsons
Research and coordination by Jessica Jones

A CIP catalogue record for this book
is available from the British Library.

ISBN 0 297 84356 7

Design director David Rowley
Editorial director Susan Haynes
Designed by Lippa Pearce
Edited by Jinny Johnson

Printed in Italy

Weidenfeld & Nicolson

The Orion Publishing Group Ltd
Orion House
5 Upper Saint Martin's Lane
London, WC2H 9EA
www.orionbooks.co.uk

# CONTENTS

# INTRODUCTION

We have no intention of writing our autobiographies so this book is the closest anyone will get to seeing inside the minds of Susannah and Trinny. You could call it our beauty biography, but this is so much more than an eulogy on particular face creams and mascara wands. We have gone into every aspect of looking good from underwear to how to lay out your wardrobe. And we have thought about the concerns that worry women throughout their lives, at different stages of their lives.

We have witnessed time and again on our television programmes and in our clothing workshops how looking good can change a woman's life. In filming our most recent series for BBC1 we have learned more about women of different ages and lifestyles than ever before. We have lived the lives of mothers with toddlers and teenage daughters, women going through a midlife crisis, the loneliness of the woman looking for Mr Commitment, and the scariness of the menopause.

In doing this we have been able to incorporate our harvested knowledge into this book and we would like to thank each and every contributor for allowing us to be them for the day. A large part of this book has sprung from these experiences because we have been able to understand how very confusing it can be for women moving on to another stage of their life, how all-consuming are the physical and emotional changes that we have to go through during the course of our lives.

We have been able here to enlarge upon those areas that are the subject of our new series – the different stages of a woman's life, the times when change can bring about a loss of confidence and feelings of inadequacy. Looking good, and feeling that you are looking good, has an important psychological role to play in moving through the five life-changing stages of a woman's life.

The first is having a baby, and in our series, we went one

step further and looked at the lives of women who have more than one toddler under five.

Having children obviously changes the way you look at yourself. Your body has become functional and no longer an expression of a sexy wife or partner. Women at this point in life suddenly find themselves needing to wear clothes for practical rather than stylish reasons. 'Is there any point in buying clothes when I don't know if I will ever be the same shape again?' is the resounding cry.

Having a baby changes a woman's body dramatically, making her feel less attractive. This in turn has a huge impact on her physical relationship with her partner which encourages a vicious circle of negative feelings. She thinks it will never be possible to regain her old life when she looked and felt fantastic. The working mother adds to these feelings of guilt and exhaustion.

As to pampering, when are you ever going to get time for a facial or even a moment to buy and apply a new lipstick? You have spent nine months in a nursing bra. Can your tits ever take anything underwired again? Your tummy has been reduced to semolina but you don't have the time to exercise or the energy to diet.

Then there is the financial side. You love your children to bits and you want to spend every last penny on them. This leaves little or nothing for you, which means having to prioritise on clothing and not making costly mistakes. The best way to combat the broke blues is to head for the No Cost Wardrobe chapter.

Looking for Mr Commitment can be a complaint common to any age. Often the reason a woman is unable to find a perfect man is because she is putting them off with her inappropriate or lack of style.

This is a sad truth, but a very real one because the shallow male fraternity are initially attracted by how a woman looks. They don't give a damn whether she's a wonderful person inside. Their first thought is of sex and what a woman will look like without her kit on.

More than for any other group in the new series, for these women it was the packaging that was the most important thing to get right. Although we knew this and had to keep it in the back of our minds, we also had to think of the women's lifestyles because they couldn't be seen looking ready to pull in the school room or the law courts.

Having said that, they had to be armed with enough appeal when walking down the aisle at Sainsbury's to attract the ideal fella browsing through the lettuces.

Overridingly with this group the problem was a lack of self esteem and feeling not good enough to be worthy of their prince. We really had to bolster our two final ladies' confidence with rousing encouragement, beautiful clothes and smouldering make-up. For one woman, in particular, make-up was anathema, something she felt she couldn't buy let alone wear because she felt so shit about herself.

We hope our work will be their salvation from loneliness… isn't it amazing what a bit of slap and a well-turned leg can potentially do.

The women in a midlife crisis seemed to have either too much or too little on their plates. It was a question of being stuck in a rut and not being able to scramble out of it. Many of the women we met used the busy-ness of their lives as the excuse to have no time to deal with their appearance.

Common to all was a general sense of panic, the realisation that maybe they had messed up their lives, of wanting to go back in time, not knowing how, realising it was impossible, and being devastated by that fact. They wanted to change, but didn't know how.

A midlife crisis seemed to manifest itself in two ways, reflected in the two women we finally chose for the series. One dressed far too young for her age, and the other had given in to frumpiness. Both suffered from a lack of identity.

Our first job was to make them look at themselves to see who they really were. This initially compounded the younger dresser's depression at not being young any more. In the case of the frump, she had to rid herself of her dowdy self-image to realise that there was an attractive woman burning as an ember within her belly core.

It was wonderful to see them both emerge as independent women excited about their futures.

Glamorous teenage daughters do highlight the fact that a woman is ageing and starting to lose her looks. It is natural that a certain amount of jealousy and competitiveness arises. It is, after all, the beginning of the next generation taking over.

If a woman has dedicated her life to being a mother, this is the point at which her role in life becomes confused. Now her daughter is getting ready to leave the nest, what is her role? Is she no longer a mother? Does she go back to being an independent woman, or a wife? Has her relationship with her husband remained strong?

How does she feel about the fact that her daughter may now be more attractive to men than she is. Does she approve of this? Does she resent her daughter?

Alongside these doubts is the awareness of how much her body is changing. Clothes she used to consider sexy may now be out of date. Does she look like mutton dressed as lamb? She wonders if she's not turning into her own mother.

And she senses that her daughter is embarrassed about her, which makes her nervous about expressing herself as a woman rather than as a mother.

This woman now has to think about focusing more on herself, not easy when the last time she did this was many years ago. Most chapters in this book will help this woman.

Of all the five stages of women being dealt with in making the new series, menopause is the one we knew least about. It was also the most depressing because so many women seem to give up once they reach menopause. They feel their life is over, that they have become invisible and are no longer making a mark in any shape or form on society.

We wanted to help give back the self esteem of every single menopausal woman we came into contact with because we know the impact looking good can make on a woman's feelings of self worth.

Here we learned about changing body shape, hot flushes, aches and pains and vaginal dryness.

And these are just the physical manifestations.

Emotionally, there is anxiety, depression, paranoia and lessening interest in sex to cope with.

What we hope we have shown in our series is that menopause is not the end of life as you know it; it is and can be the beginning of a new chapter which once accepted, indeed embraced, can be a time of freedom and rediscovery.

Your children have probably flown from the nest, you may have paid off the mortgage, and for the first time in your life your world is truly your own. This, coupled with a spanking new look in hair, make-up and clothing, can be the most rewardingly unencumbered stage of all.

The two women we finally chose started out looking as though they were closer to being topped off by a gravestone than a shock of shiny new hair. They really did feel they had come to the end of the road. It was incredible to see their determination to rejuvenate themselves once shown how to dress and groom well. They both had the will to do this and because of that our job was made so much easier.

In this book we have gone into forensic detail on all the questions, complaints and anxieties women have shared with us. We couldn't have done this on our own because we don't share every beauty and clothing problem known to woman-kind; but we have learned. In order to help women we have had to come up with a solution for dilemmas that were once alien to us but are now all too familiar.

We have investigated practically every make-up and beauty product on the market and selected the ones we feel work best for a particular purpose. We have covered the problems, and in various categories listed products that are appropriate for different age groups. The directories for these products are quite extensive – we hope it will help you through the maze of finding what is right for you.

Likewise with hair. We have sought the advice of Richard Ward, who so effectively transforms the women who have appeared on our television programmes. He has selected several of the most common hair 'situations', from how to handle frizzy hair to hanging on to long hair for too long and going grey gracefully. It's amazing what can be done with a light colour adjustment or a new style.

We have religiously avoided the *Hello!* and *OK!* spreads so here you will see the two of us pregnant and pictured with our babies.

And speaking of pictures...we will show you how to look terrific in those holiday photographs – how to sit to best effect at a table or in a swimsuit, lounge attractively on a lilo, and look a whole lot better than who or what you are standing next to.

This book is not a retouched glossy magazine account of the road to perfection. It is the honest and truthful story of how to look at yourself and see what you can make better. We are not influenced by advertising (except when it comes to coffee!) so therefore the information is first hand, tried and tested common sense.

01

# Defin
## your shape

While this is naturally the most fabulous book ever, indispensable and life changing, its information will have absolutely no effect unless you have appraised your shape. Oh God, what a vile and hideous thing to have to do. We are certain the idea of standing starkers in front of a full-length mirror makes you want to reach for the nearest plastic bowl to vomit in. We are convinced you won't want to compound the horror by making your rear view available to criticism via a hand mirror reflecting the image of your butt in the bathroom looking-glass. For sure, an order from us to do it twice in one day (morning and night) will make you wonder whether we are writing from the goodness of our hearts or a sick desire to make you feel like shit. As we have always said, deciphering your flaws and assets is a crucial part of looking your best. If you won't do it, give this book to a friend who will and watch her blossom.

It took us a long time to realise the importance of body assessment. What we conveniently forgot was the fact that our bodies had changed over the years. Faddish diets, pregnancy, exercise and lack of it had left us with bodies we no longer recognised. As the changes had happened slowly we weren't aware that our figures were no longer lithe and lean and consequently we were buying all the wrong clothes. To let you into a secret, we only put ourselves under the microscope five or six years ago. Yes, we had a good knowledge of clothes, but this only became the 'science' upon which we've built our careers after prodding and poking our parts with the precision of two neurosurgeons. And, girls, you absolutely HAVE to do this, however painful it might be.

Decoding your shape is not easy, especially as age-old misconceptions and insecurities get in the way. How do you know whether you have saddlebags, if you are an hourglass or a pear, or if your arms should be hidden at all times? It helps to do this with a good friend because the comparison will make you more aware of the way you are built. Introducing your eyes to your good points must be done in the morning before breakfast. We all feel thinner then, and more open to see what we like. The bad points become glaringly obvious at around 6pm, just as you are about to have a pre-dinner guzzle.

In both instances, take note of whether you are top or bottom heavy. Carrying the weight up top invariably means you have big boobs, fat arms, a wobbly tummy and a shorter neck, while your legs, butt and skin will be the envy of all your friends. Bottom bulk will often be topped by a long back, which means a flatter stomach because your intestines quite literally have more room. Your breasts will be smaller and your arms more shapely.

Talking legs, they too have variables and their shape and fat distribution will dictate what shoes and tights you wear. Same with a neck. If you think you look daft in a collar your neck is probably short. If thin chokers get lost, then your neck will be longer.

One time when a woman must re-evaluate her shape is during menopause. The most common change is a thickening of the waist where the stomach takes over as a main body flaw and can become bigger than your chest size. You must learn to accept your figure at every stage of your life. Look to your mother as to how you will fare at menopause.

Only when you accept your body shape will you have the courage to move on. We sympathise and know this is an awful thing to ask of you, but please take our advice – it is the first step to a new you.

# SUSANNAH

I can't believe I've ended up this shape. Although always curvaceous, the curves were where you'd expect them to be, like my waist. My tits used to be an easy to handle C. My stomach lay within my body. My arms, while strong, never required total cover. Damn it, I used to be bloody perfect. I was in proportion. Not too fat, not too thin. Now, oh my God, now things are very different. A naked Susannah is like a fat white maggot, all folds and undulating movement. The breasts have engorged to an E cup, the stomach has emerged like a hernia, open and laid out for inspection above every waistband, and the arms, well, they are worryingly vast and soon to take over my entire body. This may sound exaggerated, but it's how I feel about the parts I don't like. Luckily for me, however, I have learnt to block them out by appreciating what little there is left to love.

### My arms
I never wear sleeveless tops because my upper arms are proportionately much chunkier than my wrists. My dainty forearms become a member of the same fat family when my whole arm is displayed. This is why I cover them totally or just show my wrists in three-quarter-length sleeves.

### My tummy
To have this hanging over a too-tight waistband kills all the self-esteem I might need to get through the day. When I sit down, I always cover my belly with arms or a handy hand-bag. The best cover for my least favourite bit is a fitted top that hugs my boobs and flares out over the tummy.

### My ankles
Aside from my wrists these are the only bits of my body I am happy to show naked. Because they are thin and shapely, I can wear all skirt lengths just so long as they don't reveal my terrible, wrinkly knees.

### My neck
Weird thing to loathe, I know, but it's short and rather thick. It has no definition because it is topped by a jaw that dribbles down the gullet and makes me chinless but not a wonder. As if by magic, shirt collars erase all signs of my neck whereas round necks or polos make my face look as if I am being throttled.

### My boobs
The key to these is to keep them covered but show them off. As they are so huge compared to other parts and because my skin is now getting crepey, it's important that the cleavage line is always covered by fitted tops that still define the shape of my boobs. A lack of cleavage line makes my boobs less in your face and more demure.

### My bum
Love it. It's pert and high as a kite. I show it off at all times by wearing skirts and trousers that hug it lovingly. That way we can see that I have long legs.

# TRINNY

I grew up skinny, and never really thought about my proportions until I was an adult. Even though I am 5'10" I didn't require extra-long leg length in trousers. My tits have always been non-existent and it has never concerned me, except when I am out shopping with Susannah and rather covet her ability to hold a deep-cleavage dress in place. It wasn't until I reached my thirties that I realised I didn't look that hot in dresses, and trousers looked best with a very high heel underneath to keep me in proportion, as I tend to carry my weight on my bottom half. When I follow the rules for what to wear for my shape, I get good wear out of an item. I make new discoveries every year about how to dress for my shape; my latest is to bulk up my top half to reduce the width of my bottom. But ultimately I have to balance out how I feel inside about my shape and how others see me. The truth is somewhere in between.

**My arms**
These are definitely an asset. They have always been toned (many years of driving a Fiat Panda without power steering) and I have never been shy of showing them off. But as they are very long, I have to be careful never to wear mid-length sleeves, but most other shapes work fine.

**My torso**
I have a very long body which causes problems when I am buying tops as they are all too short. Even though my stomach is good (goes with the long back) I feel it makes my legs appear even shorter so I tend to layer clothes on my top half. I will find a top longer and in a slightly darker shade to the one I want to wear and wear that underneath. This shortens my torso and by definition elongates my legs.

**My tits**
I'm a flat-chested girl (normally flatter than this as I am still breastfeeding here) and there have been occasions when a chicken fillet filling was needed to give me some bulk on top.

**My hips**
Although skinny, I do have a bottom and thighs, saddlebags by another name. I don't look great in jeans-cut trousers in a thin fabric because they look too clingy. I am better off in trousers which are floaty or else cling over the bottom and go straight down from the widest part.

**My legs**
They are short, even though I am tall. I suffer from bad water retention so thick ankles are a permanent feature. My calves are chunky and my thighs are bulky. So I hate wearing skirts and dresses, and if I do wear either it will be over a pair of trousers so I can disguise where my bottom ends and my legs begin. In winter, boots are a godsend.

# 'I despise simplicity. It is the negation of all that is beautiful'

**Norman Hartnell**

**You need to
look at your
body. Not every
woman benefits
from over-the-
top dressing.**

'Don't believe that the only way you can feel better about yourself is by losing weight or cosmetic surgery. You can change how you look today by learning how to show off your best assets and disguise the ones you don't like.'

# 02
# Under

In the same way that a foundation stone is the basis of a building, underwear is the source for creating a well-clad body. Not only does it make or break a look, good bras and pants can also radically change the shape of your body.

You may think it extreme that a humble pair of pants can ruin an outfit. But think of Jennifer Lopez's arse, and the airtight clothes she encases it in. If her butt were kept cosy by a nice pair of comfortable knickers that didn't ride up her crack or leave room for a nasty draft between the waistline and her top, the smooth, rounded globes wouldn't be gouged by flesh-eating elastic.

Similarly bras hold (quite literally) a girl's appearance in their cups. An astonishing 70 per cent of us are wrecking our clothes with an ill-fitting brassiere. Just because it is worn underneath, its relevance, like knickers, is shunted down to the end of the style chain. It's tempting to think: 'Who cares. No one is going to see it.' Ah, ha! Not so. These undergarments can often be spotted through fabric, and if they are not, then the impression badly fitting underwear makes on flab most definitely can.

A lady we dressed recently was a case in point. Partial to a friend's clothes, she accepted all things including her B cup bras, into which she gleefully compressed her E cup tits. The result was misshapen breasts that increased in number from two to four and looked fat instead of sexy.

Your underwear is particularly important if you are looking for Mr Right. Most women think that underwear has to be sexy or supporting – you can get underwear that is both. Likewise if you are having a crisis of confidence, an easy way to feel desirable again is to invest in sexy and supportive bras and knickers. And for those women going through the menopause, it helps to re-upholster your body, rather like you would a tired old sofa!

If you are human and female you will have greying white cotton, frayed elastic, skin-digging wire poking out from bras and stained gussets littering your underwear drawer. These cannot stay. All need dispersing to the big pant graveyard in the sky. What you require girls is SUPPORT and SHAPING in all areas that have given in to gravity.

The older you get the more responsibilities you have, be it kids or mortgages. Money to burn on clothes becomes less. Surplus income should be spent on a sensible wardrobe that lasts. Well, what's the sodding point if your tits are down by your ankles and your pock-marked arse bubbles the material of your trousers. If you want to feel good, you HAVE to fork out for excellent underwear. Your hard-earned cash is far better spent on bras, pants and reconstructive fortressing than a cute top from Marc Jacobs.

Underwear, like all fashion, can fall foul of trends. There was the time when women were encouraged to burn their bras. God forbid. Then Calvin Klein came in with the compromise T shirt bra that did nothing other than obscure a nipple or two. During the late sixties and early seventies, underwear was pretty much discarded, a rebellion not only against the opposite sex but also against the constricting fifties that had us entombed in whalebone and elastic strong enough to mend a broken leg.

Nowadays, specialist knickers, tights, all-in-ones and bras are industrially enhanced for the sole purpose of improving our shape in the same way corsets did in the 19th century. Under-wiring, sucking in and winching may not be the sexiest impact upon disrobing, but it sure makes a woman feel good from the outside in.

We are passionate about the effects figure-forming underwear achieves because it gives instant gratification – it minimises the hours required in the gym and maximises the amount you can eat guilt free.

Blow the diet and exercise regime and invest in some great underwear.

# BIG TITS

Being the bearer of large breasts is not all that it's cracked up to be. They can be heavy enough to give you back problems, they make dressing elegantly a thousand times more difficult than if you have small boobs and, contrary to female belief, not all men want to suffocate during love-making.

Badly dressed breasts will ruin you. They will make you look fat and they will distort the fine line of tailoring. A big girl's worst foe can be her bra, and as most of you are wearing the wrong size there is a veritable army out there winning the war against shapely breasts.

here we go...

Anyone with a **D** cup upwards must realise
that a well-fitted bra is the most important item
in her wardrobe. Don't be scared of spending
three times as much as you would expect as
you will not regret it. If you can only afford
one bra, make sure it is made in a smooth
fabric. Avoid all lace and decoration
to broaden the bra's versatility.
Underwiring is essential as it will
push the tits forwards as well as
upwards. The jutting action alone
will make you visibly lose pounds.

# NO TITS

There is good flat-chested and bad flat-chested. If you have no tits but are blessed with an immaculate décolletage, like a virgin snow slope on a mountainside, all smooth and unmottled with no lines, you are one of the few flat-chested women who should wear deep V tops.

The rest of us, who don't have unblemished skin and probably suffer from sun damage from our teenage years, cannot. Expensive beauty products won't help either, although they can soften the skin. If you have this kind of skin you really need to ask yourself whether it's attractive enough to be on show or should you cover up and enhance your shape through clever cosmetic moulding?

But that doesn't mean resorting to a bra so padded that one does not even need to come up and take a pinch to see the fraud in your cleavage. There are alternatives. If you have a pigeon chest (where your breasts generally go in opposite directions leaving a raised crevasse in the centre), you need to fill the underneath

yeah, here they are

section with a chicken fillet to bring them back to the middle.

If you suffer from post-pregnancy deflated balloons, you need the type of support to lift and squeeze what remains into the centre without going so far in that your skin looks shrivelled.

The universally great bra for the flat-chested has to be the Wonderbra. With the ability to increase internal padding with chicken fillets and the ability to control the tightness of the cleavage with its cowboy-string device, this bra will make the best of the flattest of the flats. It is perfect for those moments when a better shape goes the longest way.

# SAGGY TITS

We find it amazing that so many women's tits hang down to the top of their knicker elastic… and that's with a bra. What's the point? Why bother wearing a bra at all if it can't combat the force of gravity. Sagging udders should be left to porky mammals slurping swill with 16 piglets attached her teats. They don't do good bras for pigs but they do for us women.

A decent shape can do the same job as a cosmetic lift allowing you to wear and look great in clothes you haven't worn since the teen years.

The ultimate bra to hoist flagging breasts is the balcony. This design lovingly cups, ups and separates your breasts to provide perfect-shaped orbs.

## yep, they're heading south

Susannah swears by it and won't even consider other varieties except when exercising or wearing a very flimsy T shirt. The beauty of having one's tits elevated is the sudden appearance of a waist. Suddenly your boobs become boobs and not the extra tyre around your middle. You look thinner, more shapely, utterly wonderful.

# FAT BACK

The bra is exquisite. Confectionery sweet and pretty as a picture. All embroidery and Belgian lace. Your tits look fabulous from the front cradled in the cups. Good enough to eat, in fact. The shoulder straps are so delightfully fine you are happy to have them peek out from under your T shirt. You assume the same about the back strap because that, too, is thread thin. The tragedy is, however, that those filament straps are acting like knives and slicing into any extra flesh you have about your back and shoulders. You might well love your tits, but do you want another pair spilling over your bra strap on your back?

If you have a podgy back, and let's face it, most of us do, you need a wide strap that will distribute the pulling power over a wider area, thus reducing the flesh-digging capabilities.

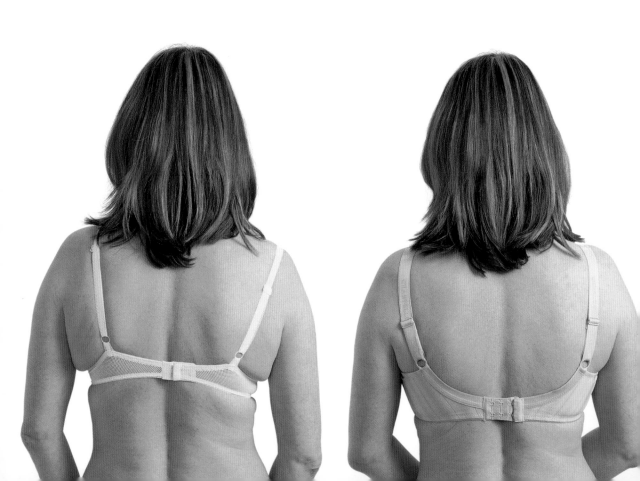

# FLABBY TUMMY

As with any waistband laid upon a fat stomach, you cannot have that of your knickers too tight. Like the bra straps, it will dig in. Frumpy and sexless though it may be, you need a waistband on your pants that reaches up to your ribcage where there is less flab. The pants are industrially reinforced by scientifically strengthened elastic.

# is the lingerie

Dorothy Parker **,**

## The more upholstery you have, the better.

S

# NO WAIST

So you thought the only way to create a waist was with the help of a belt, high-waisted trousers or a corset. Winch it in and the feminine curves arrive… well, maybe with the corset, and perhaps with the other two, but with these your body will be compromised elsewhere. A constricting belt will make you look like a knotted pair of stockings and a tight waistband will flip the flab out from underneath to create a roll which rings the entire waist. Not the right look when aspiring to an hourglass shape. The corset is very effective but hopeless when worn under a smooth, tight fabric; every whalebone will be seen.

The desired effect is one that looks seamless and the only way to achieve this is with an all-in-one body. Be sure it's made in a smooth nylon-esque fabric so that whatever is worn on top skims off it. Anything that sticks will give the game away.

# SAGGY ARSE

For a lucky few this is not an issue.
Any woman who is a pear shape will definitely
have a saggy arse (unless she is a very good
horse rider or obsessive about lunging in the
gym). In fact, for most of us there is a certain
amount of sag going on. Think of that awful
moment in the changing room with the mirrors
that allow you to see your backside: half of you
wants to see that view; the other half wishes
it wasn't there. What you don't see, you don't
have to address. Bullshit. How many people
see your behind before they see you?

The G-string is the Number One enemy of
the saggy arse. Offering absolutely no support,

it enhances and encourages gravity to pull down those butt cheeks even further. The only time to wear a G-string is under a pair of trousers with a thick fabric that in itself offers a bit of a butt lift.

The ultimate solution is a pair of contouring knickers which have built-in lift. Although seduction is then out of the question, the silhouette on offer in a pair of these condoms for the bottom will give a new lease of life to dresses and skirts once banished to the back of the wardrobe. There is always the opportunity to slip them off in the bathroom and come out pantyless (a slightly better turn-on) should that moment of seduction arrive.

# CELLULITE ARSE

How many of us have picked up a pair of gorgeous white trousers or a fab tight summer skirt, taken them to the changing room with anticipation and felt utterly despondent to discover that, once on, they were the best advert for your burgeoning cellulite. It is such a depressing yet incredibly common problem. There are creams that will fix it and diets that will help it (see Beauty chapter), but ultimately there is no better camouflage than a really great pair of latex bum and thigh knickers. Our absolute favourites are Magic Knickers.

## aaagh!

Although it might take you a good ten minutes to actually get into your Magic Knickers, the results are really worth it (see below). There is absolutely no room for the cellulite to breathe, jiggle or make its presence felt. A finish as smooth as glass covers any skin imperfections and the thinnest of fabric can slide on with confidence.

**Trinny** in her Magic Knickers.

## BIG THIGHS
## AND SADDLEBAGS

Most pear-shaped women suffer from big thighs and saddlebags, and most pear-shaped women also possess far too many bikini briefs (bought in packs of three) in their knicker drawer. Some with extra-tight white piping that grabs hold of their flesh and further enhances what they most wish to hide. Encased in a pair of too-tight trousers (with no pockets to disguise the area) the entire display reveals bodily defects in all their glory, leaving little to the imagination. Only supermodels look good in bikini briefs.

whoa

The rest of us need to take stock of our knicker drawer and really ask ourselves if what's there is doing anything for our body. Even if you are a lingerie aficionado, the satin and lace cami-knickers will do nothing for your big thighs and saddlebags. THROW THEM OUT NOW, and go and invest in a bum and thigh knicker with extra-thick lycra (see right) that will redistribute the flesh around the bum and thigh area and give you the appearance that you are thinner than you actually are.

**'** According to a leading bra manufacturer, 70 per cent of women wear the wrong sized bra. Unless you get the underwear right, all your clothes will look bad. We have never met a women with the perfect underwear in her cupboard. Check yours now. It is time and money well spent. **'**

**T̲S**

03
Colo

People who understand colour look more interesting, more in control, more confident, more self-assured and more attractive. Colour has the power to make you look healthy or unhealthy, thin or fat, short or tall. Wearing the wrong colour scheme for you could make you look like a long-term heroin abuser rather than the balanced-diet yoga queen you long to be.

And entombing your giant arse in black won't make it disappear. You'll only look slimmer if you're wearing all black. You may think this is rich coming from us, two women who avoid the funereal colour at all costs, but in this instance, it really does work...unless it doesn't suit you. Black is not the only colour that can achieve this. Any colour worn head to toe will have the same effect, as long as it's a colour that suits you.

Got up this morning feeling like shit? Don't reach for the vodka bottle, the cure lies in your wardrobe. It's amazing how wearing one of the right colours for you can change your mood from deepest darkest gloom and doom to annoyingly chirpy and effervescent.

While you need confidence to wear colour, wearing the right colour will give you that confidence. Why fit into a situation, be it at a party or at work, when you can stand out as an individual? Believe it or not, there was a time when our appearance trailed behind our personalities. Susannah had a fondness for black and white and Trinny was a smudge of mismatched pastel, which later looked like something that the cat had sicked up.

It didn't start to come together for us until we began emulating Mother Nature's palette. Instead of thinking boiled sweets, we began looking at the sunset, an autumn tree, the fire, and hey presto, things began to work. The trouble was Susannah didn't look great in her tree colours and Trinny looked dire in the colours of the dawn. We hadn't worked out our own colour groupings.

Having now dressed thousands of women we have figured out how to do this. Think yourself lucky that we've made all the mistakes in order to prevent you from doing the same.

The choice of colour in clothing is immense and therefore utterly confusing. How the hell do you work out whether buttercup yellow is your thing or aubergine should be on your butt rather than your plate? It's actually very easy, and the answer will again be in your wardrobe.

Take, for example, your favourite colour. Is it blue, red, pink, green? As we all know, there isn't just one shade of blue, red, pink or green. If it's your favourite colour you will definitely have different shades of it in your wardrobe. So let's say it's blue. You've probably got a navy, a pale icy blue, a bright blue and a sea-green blue. If Trinny were to do this test, the navy blue would wash out her complexion and give her darker circles under her eyes than she already has, and the bright blue would wear her. The pale blue would be too cold and wash her out as much as the navy, but the sea-green blue does everything to enhance her features. Her eyes look bluer, her skin looks clearer and her hair looks richer.

We've had many sleepless nights worrying over this, but after hours of brain teasing we have honed the dilemma of colour into two sections – how to pick the colours that suit you and what to wear with them. Follow these suggestions and you'll kiss goodbye to those cat sick moments.

And remember, even if your hair goes grey or you decide to change its colour in a mad, midlife crisis moment, your colour palette will always stay the same.

Menopausal women tend to stop wearing colours and shroud themselves in disappearing shades. Women with toddlers take to baby pink and baby blue. Women whose daughters have suddenly turned into beautiful young women shouldn't try to emulate their style of clothing, but they can compete on colour. This could be your chance to educate your daughter on how to wear colour.

# HOW TO WORK OUT WHICH COLOURS SUIT YOU

Go into your wardrobe and pick out the clothes in the colours you wear most often. Don't choose on the basis of whether that item of clothing actually suits your shape or if it cost you an arm or leg. This is about how the precise shade of a colour works with your face.

Take the pile to a full-length mirror in good daylight and sort by colour. Make a pile of blues, reds and so on. Taking one category at a time, put each item up against your face – and see what it does. Do your eyes look brighter? Your dark circles worse? Does your skin look radiant or does it go totally flat? You will soon know which shades of which colours are best for you.

Once you have your final pile of shades that suit you best, go to our colour charts to find out which section (Cool and Bright, Warm, or Mid Tones) you belong to. We are not looking for a perfect match here, but you should have at least four of the colours from one of the sections in your pile.

**Left** Trinny in navy; a bad choice because it does nothing for her complexion and highlights the black circles under her eyes, even though she has had a good night's sleep.
**Right** Sea green blue is one of Trinny's best colours. It lifts her complexion, brightens her eyes and complements her hair.

# HOW TO WORK OUT WHICH COLOURS SUIT YOU

Once you have established which colour category you are in, you might find that the green that is suggested is not the one you have worn before – but it will suit you more than the green in your pile.

When you have worked out your final colours, move on to our colour co-ordination pages to see our suggestions for ways to wear each individual colour (see pages 60–93).

We have taken 16 basic colours (including black and white) and shown what colours to wear with them. In all instances, the colour on the left is the basic dominant colour, the two colours next to it are ideal co-ordinates, and the colour on the right is an accent colour. This will look great as an accessory or in a scarf or detail, or as a secondary colour to wear when you are feeling extra confident.

**Left** This is one of Susannah's worst colours. It completely flattens her complexion and deadens the shine in her hair.
**Right** Watermelon is one of her best colours, bringing alive her skin, eyes and hair.

# COOL AND BRIGHT

People who suit cool colours generally have the following characteristics. When their hair goes grey it does so beautifully as a true salt and pepper, with no hint of ginger or yellow. They definitely do not have auburn hair, hazel eyes and freckly skin. Their skin is most likely to be alabaster white or olive. Their eyes have a dark rim round the iris or may be a very dark to mid brown. People in this colour spectrum look truly terrible in any type of brown; rust, dull apricot and beige are nearly as bad.

Black, on the other hand, is a good colour on you and can be worn right up to your neck; it doesn't drain your face, like it does to people who suit warm or mid tone colours. Navy works too, but to wear it in a youthful way, make sure you team it with turquoise or emerald greens.

You look great in very strong purples. Grey is one of your main colours; don't think you have to be old and fuddy duddy to wear it – it will look chic rather than ageing. If your hair has already lost its youthful colour and is on the way to being white, grey is one of your best colours.

Icy pale colours work too, but make sure they are not teamed with black as it will take all the subtlety out of them.

## You most suit

bright emerald

bright turquoise

navy

dark grey

## You least suit

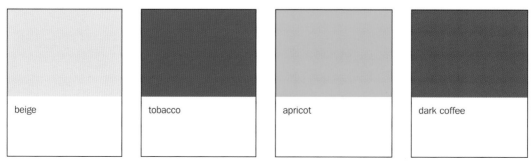

beige

tobacco

apricot

dark coffee

dove grey

blue red

schiaparelli pink

cardinal

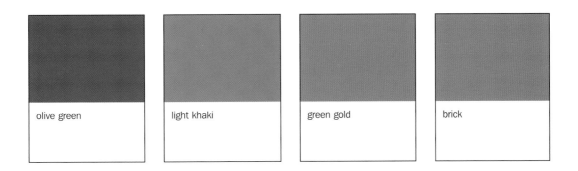

olive green

light khaki

green gold

brick

# WARM

People who fall into this category are easy to spot. The majority have some red in their hair, from rich brown through to auburn or ginger – there may even be some strawberry blondes.

When women in this category go grey, they are desperate to have their hair coloured because it can take on an unattractive hue. Their eyes might be blue, but not that bright turquoise blue; eye colour is more likely to be brown, hazel or a duller green. Their skin tone might be a little sallow or freckly, but generally not dark or mid brown.

This colour grouping looks truly appalling in black; it is their worst colour by far. Navy comes a close second, followed by any shade of pink or pastel blue. They generally do not suit colours that are cold or have too much blue in them, like a hot pink or bright turquoise. Grey is not great either, as it will totally wash out their complexion.

The best colours are autumnal – think of a New England landscape. Rusts, khakis, warm rich browns, olive greens and tomato reds. Some can wear blue if it's more of a teal blue.

## You most suit

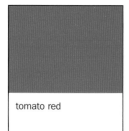

tomato red

olive

dark tobacco

sea green

## You least suit

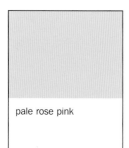

pale rose pink

hot pink

beige

icy blue

Others can get away with brick, as long as it's not too pink. You could still be a Warm and not suit apricot.

If you don't suit olive and mustard, you don't belong in the Warm section at all.

It is important to remember that Warm is the easiest category to know for sure that it's right, far more so than Cool and Bright or Mid Tones. Some people cross categories, but if you suit Warm you will definitely not be in doubt.

mustard

brown burgundy

light cream

pink burgundy

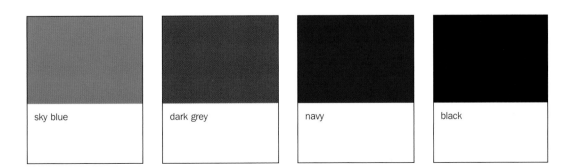
sky blue

dark grey

navy

black

# MID TONES

If you suit Mid Tones you veer towards muted bright colours. Too bright and they overwhelm you; too pastel and they take the colour out your complexion. Your skin might have blue undertones and without make-up you can appear quite washed out. At the other end of the scale, you might have a peaches and cream complexion. Your eyes are predominantly green, aqua or blue.

You look great in purples, especially wisteria and lavender. Soft blues work well, too. You can sometimes get away with navy, but your best blue is probably periwinkle. Burgundy works well, from plums to more pinkish hues. Warm pastels, like powder pink or blue, are also good.

When you are looking at your wardrobe, discard all very cold bright colours, like blue red and cardinal purple, and all colours that are

## You most suit

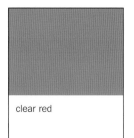

clear red

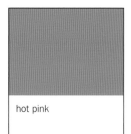

hot pink

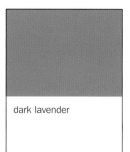

dark lavender

lemon yellow

## You least suit

rust

green gold

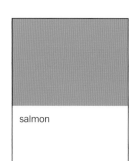

salmon

warm beige

really dirty, like beige or khaki. Your green is a sage (like the fresh, newborn leaf of an olive tree as opposed to its dying neighbour). If you are choosing purple, avoid that bright, cold tone and go for a dark lavender instead.

You will tend to wear similar tones of co-ordinating colours. If you get the colour mix right, they will make you look more alive and you will begin to see a difference. People will start to comment on how well you look and notice the colour of your eyes for the first time. But, most importantly, your wardrobe will be free of those annoying items that don't go with anything else. You will save money, you'll look great and you will no longer have to agonise over what to wear.

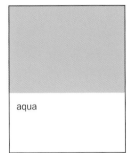

aqua

sage

mid green

periwinkle

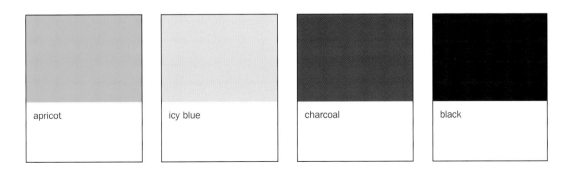

apricot

icy blue

charcoal

black

# BEIGE

Boring beige! No more. You don't have to wear beige as though you're office furniture. How about breathtaking, beautiful beige? This is one of the most versatile of colours.

Whatever your skin tone you will find a beige to suit you and whatever the occasion you can rise to it in a well put-together beige outfit. It's a sophisticated alternative to white in the summer and much more slimming.

For the evening a chic soft beige outfit will have you wafting through all the boring blacks like a celestial being. You'll make sure you're noticed without screaming 'Look at me' or dancing on the tables.

If you're one of those who can't wear grey, then beige is definitely for you and, yes, you can wear it to work, but please not head to toe or you might easily be mistaken for the filing cabinet.

Don't kill your beautiful beiges with dark brown leather shoes and handbag. Soft suede or velvet accessories are ideal.

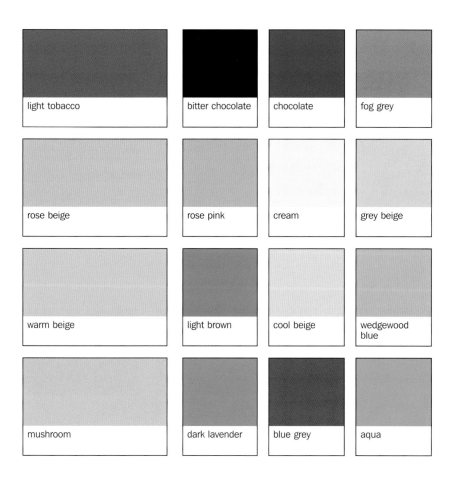

| | | | |
|---|---|---|---|
| light tobacco | bitter chocolate | chocolate | fog grey |
| rose beige | rose pink | cream | grey beige |
| warm beige | light brown | cool beige | wedgewood blue |
| mushroom | dark lavender | blue grey | aqua |

**❝ I find that this colour works best for me during the winter when my skin is at its palest. If worn with a tan it can look quite tacky. ❞**

# GREY

Grey is not a colour everyone can wear. If you have red hair, hazel eyes and a freckly skin it is not the colour for you in any shape or form. If you have deep blue eyes and black hair, or your hair is turning the type of grey you don't have to dye, then nearly any shade of grey is one of your best colours. If you are desperate to keep your hair dyed you will find grey suits you less.

A lot of people don't like grey because it was the colour of their school uniform, but it can be one of the most sophisticated colours to wear if you know how.

Grey is mostly a daytime colour, except when it's a beautiful silvery satin. It is a good alternative to black.

When wearing grey, remember that the second strongest colour in your outfit should be tonal, not too contrasting. Brighter colours can be added in smaller amounts.

A lot of people ruin grey with black accessories. Contrasting colours look best – for day, choose chocolate brown shoes or boots (suede is better than leather) and at night, high-heeled shocking pink or red court shoes.

| | | | |
|---|---|---|---|
| charcoal | dark chocolate | mushroom | shocking pink |
| dark grey | bright emerald | dark sky | dirty apple |
| steel grey | beige | steel blue | hyacinth blue |
| dove grey | lemon | lavender | eau de nil |

> **This colour grey is quite dark for me to wear if I just wore it with white. I need the warmth of the blue to carry it off. My accessories are in similar tones of dark green or turquoise.**

# YELLOW

So many people shy away from yellow because it scares them. Who would want to look like a giant custard? But yellow is also the colour of the sun so, worn correctly, it can have you stepping down the street in a blaze of glory. In general, avoid yellow if you have a sallow skin – it will make you look like a jaundice victim – but if you're black or brown skinned, tanned or even ivory, then take the plunge.

Yellow is all about how you co-ordinate it. Strong gold and buttercup yellows love hot company, such as burnt orange, tobacco and a flash of bright red. If pale yellow is your colour, go for a more demure look and team it with pale aqua and ivory, or soft orange and pale rose to create a shimmery-soft sorbet effect.

If you're still afraid, start out by wearing yellow in soft-textured fabrics like chiffon or viscose knits. These will break up the surface and be a little less attention grabbing. But if you are happy to bathe in the spotlight, yellow is for you.

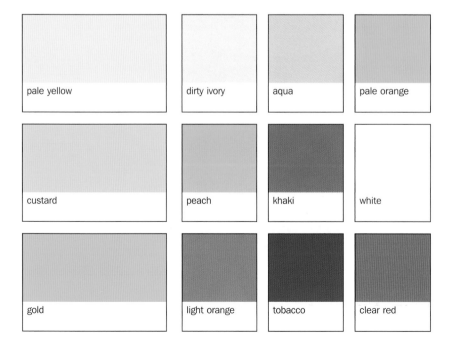

| | | | |
|---|---|---|---|
| pale yellow | dirty ivory | aqua | pale orange |
| custard | peach | khaki | white |
| gold | light orange | tobacco | clear red |

'I wear this colour when I'm at my happiest. I never seem to be attracted to it when I'm feeling low. Maybe I should because it improves my mood so much.'

# LIGHT BLUE

What's not to love about light blue? Everyone can wear it, and if you have blue eyes it's a perfect colour for you. The problem is that because light blue is so easy we often don't think – just sling it on with everything and get it totally wrong. Take a look. Is the light blue you're wearing the right blue for you?

When you're putting your blues together, think of the colours of the sea, from the warm tones of a tropical lagoon to the icy shades of a glacier, and you won't go far wrong. Many women tend to think of light blue as a sporty colour and wear it exclusively with jeans or in sweats. Well, that's okay, but why not consider an aqua evening dress? Or a powder blue suit teamed with french navy and a touch of vivid sea green?

A lot of pale blues look great with white – clean and fresh. Contrary to popular belief, they are not good with black.

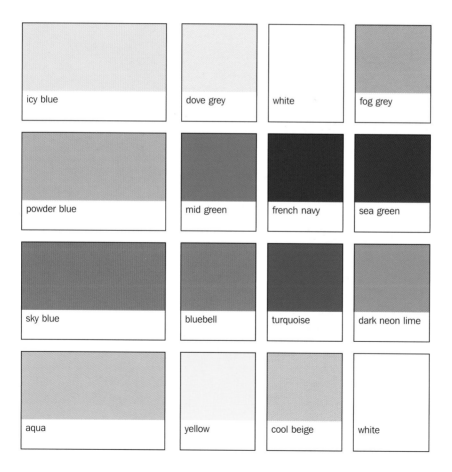

icy blue
dove grey
white
fog grey

powder blue
mid green
french navy
sea green

sky blue
bluebell
turquoise
dark neon lime

aqua
yellow
cool beige
white

> **If I were to wear a T shirt in plain pale blue, it would look terrible. The way for me to wear this colour is either to have it in a pattern with other complementary colours, like this shirt, or to wear it in a fabric with a bit of shine.**

# DARK BLUE

You might have an aversion to dark blue because it makes you feel like you've just joined the forces or been promoted to head nurse. You might even be a head nurse, but that doesn't mean you have to wear dark blue as though it's a uniform.

There are many different shades of dark blue and once you have found your shade you will wear it again and again.

In general, dark blues work well with other darker colours. Susannah, for instance, finds that wearing a brighter royal blue and a deep burgundy lifts and intensifies her french navy clothing, while a pale beige provides a sophisticated contrast.

Trinny cannot wear french navy at all, but she looks sumptuous in slate blue.

At all costs, avoid the cliché of dark blue with white – unless you're actually planning to weigh anchor and set sail.

| | | | |
|---|---|---|---|
| navy | dark purple | black | charcoal |
| french navy | royal blue | deep burgundy | pale beige |
| slate blue | sage | bitter chocolate | dark fuschia |
| periwinkle | dark lavender | grey beige | french navy |

**❝** I love this combination because it's so rich. These are the colours I wear if I feel myself veering towards black. **❞**

# DARK GREEN

'Blue and green should never be seen'…Oh, really? We say: 'Green loves blue like I love you.' Take a look at the infinite variety of landscapes where dark greens blend with blues and browns and flashes of brighter colours. Check out a peacock's tail.

Dark green is another colour that many of us avoid for fear of getting it wrong, and indeed it does require courage to make these seemingly unusual colour combinations – racing green with sea green, dark purple and mustard – look good. We promise you that they do work and if you dare to wear dark green in all its glory you will feel quite special and different in a world of navy and black.

| | | | |
|---|---|---|---|
| racing green | sea green | dark purple | dirty mustard |
| dark olive | forest green | steel blue | light orange |
| emerald | dark lime | dark aqua | deep purple |
| khaki | olive | jungle green | burgundy |

**❝** I find olive green an immensely sophisticated colour but I know others feel that it can look a bit "county". To make it work in town it needs to be teemed with something a little eccentric, like this Missoni scarf. **❞**

# PALE GREEN

For summer, pale green is ideal. It works really well with other greens, but the trick is to wear just enough green but not so much that you look like one of Robin Hood's Merry Men. And avoid wearing brown with pale green or you risk going one step further and resembling one of the trees in Sherwood Forest.

Turquoise, yellow, deep purple or even shocking pink can be great with some greens and will make sure you stand out in the forest.

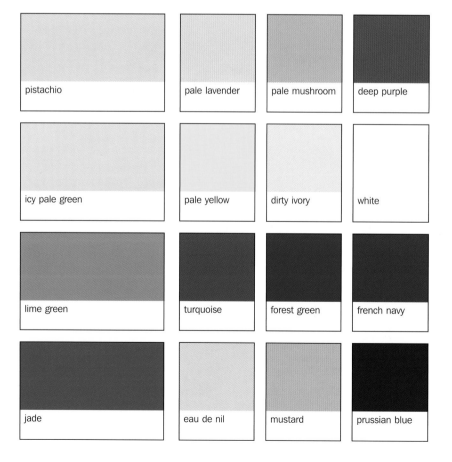

pistachio

pale lavender

pale mushroom

deep purple

icy pale green

pale yellow

dirty ivory

white

lime green

turquoise

forest green

french navy

jade

eau de nil

mustard

prussian blue

**‘** The only way I can wear a colour this bright is to combine it with a darker colour, like this navy skirt, but it still needs something extra. The rose gives a focal point which balances the stronger colours. **’**

# TURQUOISE

The fastest way to kill turquoise is to wear it with black. Yet so many of us do exactly that. This wonderful colour really comes into its own in the warm months. Trinny and Susannah have loads of it in their summer wardrobes.

During the summer, turquoise looks fabulous with beige and white and with pale greens.

Although turquoise is harder to wear in the darker days, don't overlook it as a means of enriching your winter wardrobe. Team it with navy, deep fuschia and vivid greens to create a glamorous jewel-like effect.

| | | | |
|---|---|---|---|
| sea green | bright green | emerald | aqua |
| turquoise | aqua green | lime | french navy |
| deep aqua | dirty pink | deep fuschia | apple green |

> **❝ I suit a very deep turquoise, nearly green, which doesn't actually work with white. It looks its best when teamed with darker, stronger colours. ❞**

# PURPLE

From the palest lilac to the deepest plum, find the purple that's yours and then work it in throughout your wardrobe. Do try to avoid dressing entirely in purple, though. This is strictly the preserve of bishops.

Purple makes an excellent base colour as it's easy to match and works in so many ways. Wear it sedately with olives, burgundies and deep green, or add pizzazz with fuschia, strong pinks and even orange. The wearing of purple was once restricted exclusively to royalty and it's still a symbol of all that's luxurious.

Purple is a really good alternative for those who can't wear burgundy, and it's just so much more regal than navy blue.

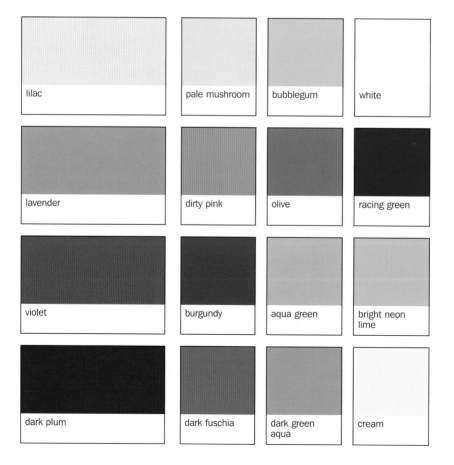

| | | | |
|---|---|---|---|
| lilac | pale mushroom | bubblegum | white |
| lavender | dirty pink | olive | racing green |
| violet | burgundy | aqua green | bright neon lime |
| dark plum | dark fuschia | dark green aqua | cream |

**Colours that are too dark tend to wash out my face so I've chosen my best green to lift the purple and lend an added richness to the velvet.**

'
when in
wear re

not if it doesn't suit you. 5

# doubt

## d...,

Bill Blass

# RED

'I can't wear red.' Well, you may be right.
Red is difficult to wear and you really must find
the right tone for your complexion. If you have
even a touch of the florid in your skin, if you are
just slightly sunburned or a fake tan devotee,
red will only bring out the lobster in you.

Surprisingly, red can look its very best against
pale white skin or black skin, as well as with the
beige skin tones.

The trick with red is to keep it hot. Wear it
with pink and orange and tobacco and fuschia.
There's no point trying to tone down red. Pump
it up. Wear it full blast or don't wear it at all.

The most common mistake is to team red
with black or white, or both. Don't do it.

| | | | |
|---|---|---|---|
| tomato | tobacco | brick | dusty pink |
| raspberry | hot pink | fuschia | violet |
| blue red | shocking pink | bright orange | plum |

**This is the only red that I have in my wardrobe. Solid red just wears me but broken up into this pattern, with the pink tones further brought out by the necklace, I can just about get away with it.**

# BURGUNDY

If burgundy is your colour, like it is mine, then you have hit the jackpot in making colour co-ordination easy. Burgundy is endlessly versatile. I love it with all shades of pink and flame-inspired oranges and reds.

It breaks my heart when I see this rich colour deadened by navy blue or black. It is, however, a great alternative to black because it is dark and makes you feel slim.

Burgundy can be a very ageing colour if it is too dull and cold a shade, or if you have warm-toned skin and hair. It particularly suits an olive skin.

Do not wear black accessories with your beautiful burgundy outfit. If you don't have a pair of burgundy, fuschia pink or rust-coloured shoes in your wardrobe, go for chocolate brown or olive green.

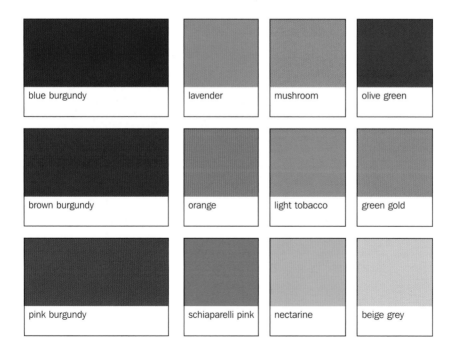

| | | | |
|---|---|---|---|
| blue burgundy | lavender | mushroom | olive green |
| brown burgundy | orange | light tobacco | green gold |
| pink burgundy | schiaparelli pink | nectarine | beige grey |

**ＬＬＬ** When I wear this outfit I feel good. It can make a tired face look a bit chirpier because these colours bring out my features the best. I can be pale or tanned and it will still look good. Missoni is one of the best designers when it comes to understanding how to put colours together. **▋▋**

# ORANGE

Orange is much more forgiving than red, but it can still be difficult on pinkish skin tones. If you are of a rosy complexion, choose your orange with care, but if you have a suntan or you are olive or black skinned, go for it.

In summer you can be a riot of glorious orange light, like Van Gogh's sunflowers, and in winter you can be as warm as a log fire blazing in a brick hearth. These are the tones to look for (not those from a fizzy drink).

Almost every shade of orange has its complementing shade of pink; they were pretty much born for each other.

Orange, rust and tobacco are good colours for accessories to wear with orange and they are a livelier alternative to brown.

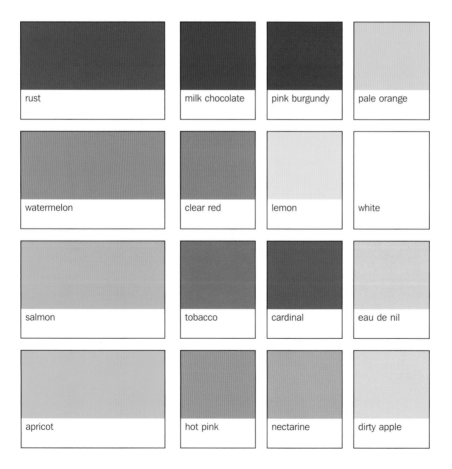

| | | | |
|---|---|---|---|
| rust | milk chocolate | pink burgundy | pale orange |
| watermelon | clear red | lemon | white |
| salmon | tobacco | cardinal | eau de nil |
| apricot | hot pink | nectarine | dirty apple |

**❝ I can never wear orange around my face but I'm always drawn to it as a very happy colour. It looks great with this burgundy which is one of my favourite colours. ❞**

# PINK

When you were a little girl, did you go overboard on pink?

And have you now banished it from your life forever and replaced it with the dark forces of purple and black? But if your wardrobe is still overflowing with pink, we can bet that you are wearing lots of shades that don't suit you.

First, get out each garment and do the colour test. Do you see a breathtaking vision or just a blancmange? Not sure? Ask your ruthless friend. Then look at our colour charts to find colours to enhance and co-ordinate with your shade of pink – apart from pink.

If, on the other hand, you are an undercover goth who wouldn't be seen in your coffin wearing pink, then we feel that you are really missing out. Pink can be hot and sexy, and the softer shades are very appealing to the eye.

rose quartz    icy blue    pistachio    pale taupe

nectarine    pale brick    dull apricot    mushroom

bubblegum    purple    orange    forest green

schiaparelli pink    dark orange    light orange    dark eau de nil

**‘** Deep pink is a colour I wear far more in the summer; the winter sees me running back towards burgundy. **,**

# BROWN

As with grey, a lot of women won't wear brown because it was the colour of their school uniform. If you are not wearing brown you're really missing out because there is a beautiful brown for nearly everyone.

When you think of brown, don't think 'detention', think cappuccino, chocolate, camel, sand, biscuit, tan, tobacco, mink, terracotta, puce, mahogany and…sable.

The only women who have difficulty wearing brown are those who suit very cool colours, generally those with pale, pale skin and dark blue eyes or the darkest tones of black skin.

Most browns will look elegantly understated worn with the right tone of grey, while dark browns always look stylish with black. Warmer browns are great with green gold and also rust.

Brown is also a really useful colour for accessories. Brown leather, in particular, looks richer and more expensive than black and is far more versatile in working with the other colours in your wardrobe.

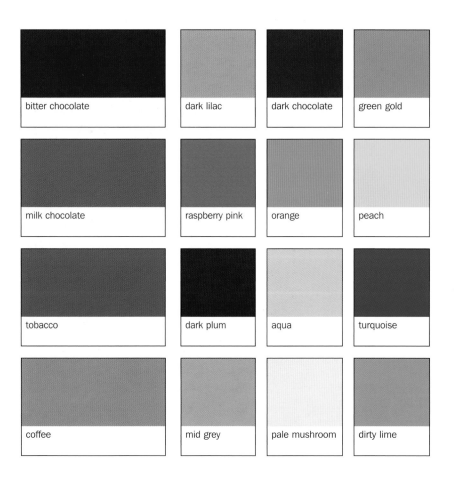

| | | | |
|---|---|---|---|
| bitter chocolate | dark lilac | dark chocolate | green gold |
| milk chocolate | raspberry pink | orange | peach |
| tobacco | dark plum | aqua | turquoise |
| coffee | mid grey | pale mushroom | dirty lime |

> **Dark brown on its own, especially in wool, washes me out. The solution is to wear it in a luxurious fabric like velvet which gives an added richness, making it wearable for me.**

# WHITE

Mistake number 1: almost everyone thinks that white is just one colour.

Mistake number 2: almost everyone buys every shade of white and thinks it will suit them because 'it's just white'.

White can be sharp and bright or it can be warm and creamy – ecru. You have to find the shade that is right for you.

If bright white suits you, it will have a wonderfully uplifting effect on a tired day, lighting up your eyes and giving a natural reflection to your face. But if it is not your colour, it will totally wash you out.

Once you have found your white, go out and buy several fitted white T shirts in that shade (taking care that they are the right cut for your body shape). This is every woman's essential item for dressing down a smart skirt, wearing with jeans, under blouses and tank tops, with sweats.

A word of warning: chunky white cotton knits only look good on Ralph Lauren models.

A second word of warning: in our opinion, the biggest fashion crime is the round-necked, loose-fitting, half-sleeved, white polyester blouse. If you own one of these, burn it.

| white | mushroom | light cream | warm beige |
| light cream | pale rose pink | pale green gold | pale orange |
| cream | pale eau de nil | pale peach | pale dirty pink |

" Bright white, apart from reminding me of my school shirt, is a colour that really drains me, yet ecru (a much warmer white) can really lift me and make my skin glow. It's amazing how such a small variation in colour makes such a big difference to how I look. "

# BLACK

Black is not a colour. It is an absence of colour. It is a drama, a pool of nothingness, a depth.

Do not treat black lightly. It is not a background for bright colours, nor is it a catch-all shade for shoes, handbags and dreary suits.

Black goes with black, and that's that. Okay, you may team it with brown for chic winter daywear, or with flashes of gunmetal or dove grey for special evenings, but those are our only concessions.

Black is the most abused and misused colour (or non-colour) of them all. It should be reserved for high occasions and funerals; instead, it is worn in offices, shops, bars and restaurants the length of this land. Black has become the tedious uniform of modern Britain. We now call upon you to banish black from your working life.

If you treat black with the respect it deserves, it will repay you by endowing you with all the glamour and mystery of a first lady or film star.

| black | white | dove grey | steel grey | bitter chocolate |

**' I can't wear black on its own. I wish I could. But I can wear it with my grandmother's fur stole. '**

'You might not think that you suit a certain colour, but there will always be a shade that will suit you. Don't be lazy and only wear colour with black; open up your imagination and wear colour with colour.'

TS

04

Culling

Look in your wardrobe and what do you see? Rows of clothes you wear every day because you love them all; each and every item? Neatly hung garments that hold your admiration because they all look fabulous upon your form? Like hell you do. We bet millions that the more likely scenario is one of shelves littered with kit that hasn't been worn for eons.

Don't think we don't know about the knickers that have greyed in the wash and can't stand up for themselves because the elastic has gone. Don't lie about those sweaters. We know they hold more holes than the Hutton Report. Oh Lord! Now look at those dresses. They haven't seen daylight for years, but their garish colour schemes have not faded at all. And check out the shoes. You know full well that you will never get that heel fixed and the scuffed toes of your boots are beyond polish salvation. Your first boyfriend may have given you the spray-on jodhpurs with suede patches. They remain hideous and you can't even get into them. Sure your navy winter coat cost a week's wages and has a designer label, but that doesn't take away its exaggerated lapel and dandruff-embedded shoulders.

When your hair gets too long and the ends become split ridden you get it cut. If your appendix explodes you have it surgically removed. Well, the same has to be done with your clothes. What is the point of cluttering up your cupboards with things that are never worn, be they there for sentimental reasons or financial ones? If they aren't worn, they aren't worn. Get rid of the buggers.

Culling is relevant to every stage of a woman's life, and particularly for women going through the menopause, who may hold on to clothing from the time they felt their most feminine and sexy. Get these clothes out of your wardrobe; they will only depress you. And then you can get something new to replace them.

If you are looking to meet Mr Right, get rid of those clothes that make you look like you've always got your period. You never know when you are going to meet him so even the most casual outfit must be well thought out. Mr Right might be walking down the supermarket aisle.

As a good culling is no easy task, it does help to have a friend help harden your resolve. She can confirm that white lace in your case is for Victoria sponges. And she will persuade you to get rid of those leather trousers that sag at the bum. All is not lost, however, because those less fortunate than you can benefit from the funds raised by selling those old skirts and jackets in charity shops, and your appearance will benefit from newer and more expensive things being sold to raise funds for a shopping spree.

Bagging old clothes is like casting out baggage from your past. It is a cathartic process that will make you feel cleansed and renewed. And there is no down side to culling because for every six or so items you discard there will be another you find among the rubble that can be worn with the pride of a spanking new purchase.

While some pieces deserve nothing better than a bin liner, others could look well among the charmingly dated merchandise unique to charity shops. These you'll get no cash for (obviously), but send the more with-it items to a second-hand store and your financial reapings could be significant enough to buy a new coat. Anything over a decade old, in good order and preferably with a designer label attached will find a wealthy home on ebay or in a vintage shop. Making money from your cast-offs eases the agony of saying goodbye to old friends (even if they have been stabbing you in the back by making you look ghastly).

Go back to the war-zone that is your wardrobe, take a deep breath and dive in.

# BRAS

We bet that there are more redundant bras in your drawers than anything else. This is because your bust is more susceptible to size fluctuation than any other part of your body. Think of pre-period, pregnancy and weight gain or loss. Fit is immeasurably important. If your tits spill over the top, the straps dig into your skin, it's turned grey, the underwire is poking out or it is nothing more than a nipple shield, chuck it.

**yuk!**

# KNICKERS

The G-string gives VPL freedom. Low-waisted shorty shorts are great for jeans, but bikini briefs and cami-knickers along with any granny pants aren't flattering and can go, together with anything discoloured or gaping with loose elastic. If your pants are clean, fresh and invisible, you are clean, fresh and confident.

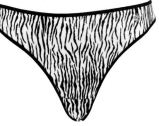

# SWIMWEAR

Try on all your swimwear and get rid of any orphan pieces, anything that doesn't fit or is stretched beyond redemption. If your body has been ravaged by childbirth, maybe it's time to put two pieces behind you. A smart one piece can look wonderful.

# JUMPERS

The culling candidates here are numerous. And also the hardest because a jersey is warm even if it is peppered with moth holes. But it will be better given to a needy vagrant who can keep out the cold without worrying about how it looks. A sweater should always have shape, no matter what your size.

# T SHIRTS

We always need that holiday souvenir and the pop concert memory. We need one to go with jeans, one for under a jacket. Some for exercising, some for sleeping. Whatever, we all have far too many. You don't need the baggy, the too-tight white or the one attacked by red boxer shorts in the wash. Stick to T shirts that suit your shape, a few white, a few colours and motifs. Ten should suffice.

## SKIRTS

Being more of a headline garment, skirts are harder to dump. To be honest, once you have found your favoured shape there really should be no need to eject them unless the hardware has been hit, like a zip or a hook and eye. Summer holiday skirts (gorgeous colours and wafting fabrics) can go on forever. Get rid of anything that's been splashed by wine, anything that's too short or requires a petticoat, and most definitely anything with an elastic or gathered waist.

# in the

## TOPS

Other top-half garments that should be binned: the classic but-no-longer-white shirt, the silk top (fine for flat chests or the mature lady) and halternecks (unless you have the skin of a 12 year old). Keep waistcoats well hidden when they're out of fashion.

# bin please!

We feel a short coat is a better investment than a jacket, unless it's a useful waterproof or sports jacket. The price is usually much the same, and it's a more modern look. Bin anything that has even the remotest sheen from too much dry cleaning, anything with big shoulders or a blouson style, and certainly bomber and biker jackets – sooo unflattering. Leather jackets can stay if they are fitted, and jean jackets (the older the better) too, unless they are stone washed.

# HATS

These are probably in competition with your oldest bras for the least-used items in your wardrobe. By all means keep your favourite sun and sporting hats. All the others that have been gathering dust at the top of your wardrobe should go – the picture hat, the beret, the trilby and anything you bought in the eighties and haven't worn since. That doesn't mean you shouldn't wear hats; just re-evaluate what suits you, and update. There is never a reason to wear a baseball cap.

# TROUSERS

Our least favourite trouser has pleats at the waist and tapered legs which end at the ankle. And it's usually black too. Get rid of it, or them, immediately. And bin any jeans which are stone washed, drainpipe, studded or way too tight. You've probably got several pairs you no longer wear taking up valuable space in your wardrobe.

# COATS

If you live in a cold climate you will wear this item proportionately more often than any other in your wardrobe, so think about updating it accordingly. If you have the perfect coat that's simple, stylish and elegant, then look after it, along with the stylish vintage evening coat if you are lucky enough to have one. Anything that's shapeless, moth-eaten or worn should go.

eeek!.

# 'Make do and mend'

Second World War poster campaign

# Only if there's a war on.

# SCARVES

Shawls, cashmere pashminas and realistic imitation fur scarves are warm and therefore have a purpose. Everything else needs close inspection before you consider keeping it. There's absolutely no reason to keep the thin velvet or chiffon scarf, the synthetic 'angora', the chenille, and alas, the square silk scarf presently out of fashion for anyone except the elegant older woman.

# GLOVES

Another candidate for a cull at the end of each winter. Gloves have a habit of getting rained upon, being the only thing to hand when you have a runny nose, shrivelling up, and developing holes in the tips. In all cases, anything that's not in good condition should be culled. And remember to dry clean the ski gloves.

## SHOES

If it's too small, too high or uncomfortable, there's a heel missing or the leather is terminally scraped, the inner sole is buckling or, worse still, it smells, out it goes. The same applies to ancient trainers and those expensive evening shoes that don't go with anything in your wardrobe.

And check that what you keep is the right shape for your leg.

## BAGS

We don't believe in the bag-for-each-outfit way of thinking, but we do believe the one-bag-for-all-occasions is completely wrong. The kitchen sink bag is unsightly to look and bad for your back. It's time to wave goodbye to some other old friends too – anything that lives out of sight (and out of mind) in the top of the cupboard, anything that's stained, frayed or just plain dirty, as well as anything that is quilted, has a gold chain or was a make-up freebie.

## EVENING GOWN

It cost a fortune at the time and you have worn it twice (the last time ten years ago). It's sexy, but a little tight, or a bit too short. It's got frills or eighties beading. If any of the above apply, it's out. If there's something you really love and it looks great but is stained, try having it dyed a darker colour.

# scary!

## DRESSES

Our least favourite is the raucously coloured dress that ties at the back and makes you look like a sack of potatoes. Uggh. Be ruthless and cull the mistakes you made looking for the right-shaped dress in the right colours for you.

# JEWELLERY

Most of us have boxes of impulse buys dating back to our teens, and much of what's in them doesn't stand scrutiny today. If you haven't bothered to replace the missing stone

or restring the broken necklace, out it should go. Any intact pieces can go into the children's dressing-up box or to charity. Keep the charm bracelets for the next generation.

'Don't do this alone. Make sure you have a friend to harden your resolve. If she's not your shape, so much the better - or she will want the clothes.'

# 05
# No cost wardrobe

This chapter is most relevant for women with toddlers and teenagers. Because you are always thinking of giving everything to the kids, there is nothing left in the kitty for yourself. Stop just being a mum. You are still a wife or partner, and it's important that you don't dress just for practicality. You may not be able to afford new clothes, so this is the ideal solution.

One assumes increasing the contents of one's wardrobe means spending money on new clothes. Over the years, however, we have discovered that many of the clothes worn by us actually look better on friends whose body parts are correctly developed to take a certain shape or style of clothing. You may desire the asset of another woman, but woe betide that physical trophy if it's adorned in something it doesn't suit. The enlarged chest Trinny may desire will look awful in a polo neck, but because she is as flat as a freshly pressed ski slope the roll-neck sweater becomes an altogether more elegant item upon her torso whereas it is not a possibility for Susannah.

In the old days we were always buying kit that was better for each other. It took a while for the penny to drop that Susannah looked atrocious in the strappy dresses Trinny encouraged her to buy. This wasn't evil intent on Trin's part. She genuinely loved the dresses. When Susannah, enchanted by killer heels with ankle-cuffs, implored Trinny to take them, this was not a secret stab in the back, but a desire to see Trinny as happy as she would have been could her bank balance have absorbed the price tag. Back in those days we were ignorant of the fact that what was captivating to one of us was cataclysmic when put on the other. Once the bulb lit, we began swapping clothes.

This very basic fact leads on to an extremely profitable plan in terms of gathering clothes for nothing. Invite a bunch of girlfriends round for dinner along with a selection of their clothes. Try on each other's kit. Be ruthless in your assessments (especially if criticising something you know will look better on you). Things that don't suit you can be donated to a properly shaped friend in exchange for something of hers you look great in and she didn't.

This exchange should not be about labels and prices. In order to make the event equal and not about money, each girl should remove the labels of her clothes before she attends the party. This will also make people desire the clothes rather than the label and make objective choices. It's an obvious idea, but a good one that really does allow you to walk away with some new outfits without a single penny exchanging hands.

This is especially good for friends who might have a vast wardrobe that could come winging your way, but it is equally satisfying to help a friend with less money than you without making her feel like a charity case.

You might also be hanging on to your thinner-day clothing in the vain hope that one day it will fit you again. Let it go in the knowledge that what goes around comes around, and if and when you lose that weight the universe will always provide.

Swapping clothes is also a great way to obtain and get rid of a pregnancy wardrobe. You won't feel so guilty about the black tie dress you spent a fortune on and only wore when you were pregnant.

You might be holding onto an item because of its sentimental value; if you love it so much, give it a new lease of life and see the joy it gives to a friend rather than let it hang unworn in your cupboard. At the end of the day it's about friendship.

Every woman has screaming mistakes in her wardrobe which we try to ignore by pushing them into the back recesses where they fester in the vain hope of being worn. It's never going to happen, appease your guilt and get rid of them NOW.

'If you've wear

# got it,
## it'
### Lord Mountbatten

**But if it looks better on your best friend, give it to her.** $\overline{s}$

# List of friends

## Things I would like to get rid of

_____

_____

_____

_____

_____


## Things I would like to get

_____

_____

_____

_____

_____

**"** We all know retail therapy is the best kind, but there will always be times when we can't afford it. You don't have to spend money to get new clothes. **"**

06
Access

The quickest and most effective way to accomplish a stylish appearance is with accessories. But like anything that works wonders, there is no shortcut to learning how to accessorise well.

While we have always said style isn't innate, there are women to whom the art of knowing how to use accessories comes easily. They will inherently know which shoes to put with a particular length of skirt and how a necklace can make or break an outfit. Those of us deprived of the accessory gene need to be taught what to do.

Deciding which types of accessories suit you depends very much on the shape and size of your bones. Forget about how much you weigh for once – it is your bones we want to focus on.

Look at us as an example. Susannah is podgier than Trinny (except on her arse), but because she is fine boned, she suits more delicate accessories. Thin Trin, on the other hand, is blessed with heftier bones that can carry off bold accessories, which in turn stand out more.

While we admit this bone thing is, of course, a sweeping generalisation, and there are always exceptions to the rule, it's a starting point to a subject that will change your attitude to dressing.

How on earth can you tell what is a big or a small bone? Well, the difference isn't enormous. We are not talking brontosaurus excavation site versus wren skeleton here. No, the definition is more subtle. Look at your wrists and ankles and if these are proportionately delicate to the rest of your arms and legs, then your bones are small. If, however, the two are less distinct and you have, for example, thick ankles, your prize is that you can wear fabulously daring pieces which people comment on. Hands, too, are a strong indicator to sizing accessories. Do your fingers look better in big or small rings?

Personality plays a part as well. No shrinking violet, however enormous her bones, is going to want to stand out with an accessory that screams, 'Look at me!'

The bottom line is big characters have the balls to go bold or fragile, whereas the reserved may want to play safe with subtlety.

Think the learning process stops here? Well, interestingly, clothes do play a part, too, especially when it comes to colour. Keeping your accessories in tune with what you wear is vital, however important a piece is. The thing you love most about an outfit may be the necklace that you wear with it because it is a most individual item. Even in this instance, your clothes need to be of a similar colouring but of an unfussy fabric and pattern which will make the necklace stand out. The tone you set also makes a difference. Diamanté in the daytime looks cheap, but it comes into its own at night.

We also firmly believe less is more. Someone who wears her entire jewellery collection about her person does not look rich and classy but desperate to be seen as rich and classy.

It might be that the season's hottest look is military or flamenco. Unless you have either a boyish form or a curvaceous Latin American one you can't go there in terms of clothes.

You can, however, make great use of a gold button or two, or the rose that looks so good on a Spanish dancer in full regalia; it would look just as wonderful pinned to the lapel of your jacket.

Once you know your style, but want to be fashionable, give more attention to the runway shoe when looking through glossy magazines. You can pick up super-trendy footwear from high street stores at a fraction of the cost of the originals.

# BEST BAGS

A woman can never get away with just one 'useful bag'. What will she do when she goes to the ball, wears different coloured clothes, gets on a plane or goes down to the beach? There are many occasions when we need a bag, and for each of these we should have at least one example. So if you are that girl who owns only a practical navy shoulder bag, it's off to the shops you must go.

Here is your list for an ideal bag collection.

• Day bag in brown. This will be worn with all colours apart from black, though ideally we would like you to get a few different colours.

• Day bag in black. Not as useful, funnily enough, as the brown, because you can only wear it with black, white, grey or taupe.

• Funky fabric bag. Dotted with a few beads or flowers, this is great for playtime and when you're going out for dinner.

• Evening bag. Best to get this to match up with your jewellery. If you like diamonds, get a silver bag, and if you are a gold girl, get a gold one.

• Travel bag. One that will fit in the overhead locker of a plane. This will double up as a weekend bag.

• Beach bag. Preferably lined in something that can be wiped clean when your sun cream leaks or water seeps into it.

• No bag bag. A bag that is little more than a wallet for the days when you need carry only the bare essentials, like keys, card and phone.

# BAGS

It is so easy to ruin an outfit with the wrong bag.
So many women assume that one bag fits all.
It truly doesn't. Heavy, dark-coloured bags may
look fine with your winter coat but they will
overwhelm a floaty summer outfit. And you don't
always want to carry your practical work-day
number at the weekend.

**Below left** Susannah's bag is nice enough, but dull and mumsy.
**Below** The novel shape of this bag adds an element of fun.

**Opposite left** The heavy black bag completely swamps Trinny's dress.
**Opposite** The pink bag is prettier and more in proportion with Trinny and the dress.

# KITCHEN SINK BAG

A busy woman needs to carry her life in her bag, so it needs to be big if it's going to hold the contents of her daily routine. It might rain, so there's an umbrella. She might be called upon for a sudden meeting so there's her diary/notebook. She might have to dash straight from the office to the dinner table, so there's the hefty make-up to reapply her face. Sod's law she'll have her period at the same time. Her big bristly hairbrush will also be included because it's the only one she has. If she has children, there will probably be a stray nappy or half-empty bottle of baby milk in there too. All that's missing is the proverbial kitchen sink, but of course there's no room for that.

If you are that woman, it's time to think mini. Buy small sizes of make-up and beauty products or decant them into miniature containers. The brush can be shrunk to a few inches that will do the job just as effectively as the big fella. Cull all unnecessary items. You can get tiny, light umbrellas, and how about an electronic organiser instead of a heavyweight diary?

What a joy it will be to have easy access to your life by getting rid of the chaos that was once the contents of your handbag.

**Below** Before and after handbags.

**Above** Contents of the kitchen sink bag.
**Right** Revamped mini contents for the new, organised you.

# HATS

Hats have fallen by the wayside over the past few decades. Once upon a time, they used to be the icing on an outfit's cake. No woman nor man would have walked out of their front door without donning a little chapeau of some kind. Right up until the end of the 1950s hats continued to be a feature when out in public. A hat was evidence of a person's decorum. Hats commanded respect for the wearer and looked wonderfully elegant at meal times when all ladies of consequence would keep them on, in spite of the handicap they must have imposed when trying to stuff a cucumber sandwich into the mouth.

By the 1960s hats had ceased to be obligatory. They were relegated to the rank of accessory, an item to be worn when desired, but no longer an essential part of the overall outfit.

Back in those heady days of innate elegance a woman knew how to wear a hat. She knew whether her face was suited to an upturned brim and when a small hat was more appropriate than a picture version. Today we have not a clue. Yes, we are aware that people turn up to a wedding wearing a hat, but that is the only occasion we feel duty bound to put one on, aside, perhaps, from a day at the races.

But don't be scared of hats. They shouldn't be just for weddings and race days. A casual hat can be the saviour of a bad hair day.

These rare sightings of hats, like spotting an animal on the verge of extinction, has increased their importance. The average woman will probably buy only two or three hats in her

**Below left** Susannah's small-brimmed hat is wrong for the shape of her face.
**Below right** She needs a wide brim to give proportion to her face and shoulders and to flatter, not enlarge, them.

lifetime so will want to make sure she chooses the right ones. If you can find the shape that suits you, an investment hat should last you for life. We have worked this out by trial and error.

Looking back at family snaps of ourselves we have been only too aware of the hats that enhance our features versus the ones that turn us into sad sacks.

There are a few other helpful pointers:

• High foreheads can wear beanies.

• Low foreheads (like Susannah's) can only wear high-crowned hats. Anything else turns the face into a bloated blow-up, all fat features and nothing else.

• High foreheads get away with more or less any style of hat, but people with these do have a tendency to be burdened with eye bags.

These must never be shadowed by a low brim because two words – Grim and Reaper – will immediately spring to mind.

• If you are one of the front pew party at a wedding, think before you choose a huge hat. You'd probably block the view of everyone behind you.

• Downgrade a smart trouser suit with trainers and a beanie.

• If you have to buy a hat for a special occasion, invest in one that is truly spectacular. If you are only going to wear the hat a couple of times, be sure to do it well.

• The smaller the brim, the more casual the hat, unless it is shaped like a piece of sculpture or bedecked with assorted bits from the haberdashery department.

**Below left** Trinny disappears under this high-crowned, small-brimmed hat.
**Below right** Her best style has an up-turned brim which exudes elegance and shapes and complements her face.

# HATS

With the relaxing of the dress code and demise of any rules of etiquette, hat makers have adapted their skills to incorporate things that look like hats but actually aren't. As more women cotton on to the ease with which these hair accessories can be assembled, you now see flowers and feathers put together to create hat-like headgear that is cheap to buy and glamorous to wear.

If your face is small, keep the flowers as close to it as possible. Anything placed towards the back or on top of the head will look precarious and as though it is stuck on.

Floral accessories are incredibly versatile. Take a couple on holiday and you'll find yourself wearing them on the beach, at the bar and pinned to your dress.

Flowers are especially good on dark hair. They bring out the señorita in your soul.

**Below** These styles are unconventional but will look both modern and fun at a wedding.
**Opposite** If you don't want to go the full hat route, you could try wearing a flower in your hair to add a touch of glamour for a special occasion.

# GLOVES

What is the point of gloves? Nobody wears them apart from Her Majesty, old ladies and frozen fingers in the cold winter months.

The irony is that is a pair of well-chosen gloves can round off an outfit beautifully and turn a smart look into something nearing perfection.

What do you do if you are off to a meeting be-suited and chic and the temperature falls to sub zero? Don a pair of gaudy mittens knitted by granny? Shove your frozen digits into muffly sheepskin? Resort to your ski gloves because they are the only gloves you own? Or, most likely, dig out your faithful navy or black leather gloves that are as warm as a condom and as stylish as surgical rubber stabbing a gall stone. Leather is absolutely fine, but all the more beautiful when worn in fabulous colours that complement what you are wearing.

Evening gloves are favoured by those who think they add a touch of class to their ball gown. In truth, the opposite applies, unless of course you are off to the palace, where the dress code is White Tie.

**Left** A perfect example of when gloves are not needed.

Trinny's outfit is smart already, but becomes very smart indeed with the addition of striking orange gloves.

# SCARVES

Scarves, believe it or not, come in many different guises and can give off a variety of impressions. You can make any scarf look funky – or Meals on Wheels.

The answer to good scarf-wearing lies in the way it is tied. A silken square knotted far back under the chin can immediately turn a young woman into a zimmer frame-pushing old dear who smokes 50 fags a day. The very same scarf knotted ON the chin belongs to a county hooray whose fashion role model is Princess Anne. If this same silken square is worn as a wide headband from the hairline back, around a pair of jeans, or tied to a Marc Jacobs-style bag next to worry beads or a cool key ring, it suddenly becomes non-stereotypical and rather hip.

A few hints on scarf wearing:

• Look out for unique scarves in vintage stores.

• A Missoni scarf can teach you about colour because this design house really understands how to combine complementary hues.

• If you are short and yearn for a long scarf, don't be lured into wearing one in a thick knit; opt for a light-weight material or woven silk.

• A scarf is fab worn as a belt with jeans.

- If your hair needs a wash, cover it up in a scarf worn hair-band style à la Elizabeth Taylor in the sixties.
- Short necks must wear scarves wrapped round the neck to create an elongating polo neck effect.
- Long necks can wear scarves looped and tied.
- Scarves folded in a triangle and placed over the shoulders like a cowl are very Bus Pass.
- A cotton kerchief tied round the neck and worn with a T shirt makes for a fresh French feel that works for all ages and is a nice alternative to the hideously tied Sailor Boy knot.
- The scarf worn like a choker is the saviour of wrinkly turkey necks.

**Opposite left** Susannah's scarf is wildly out of proportion with her size.
**Opposite right** The scaled-down version, wrapped round her neck, is the right size and a good style for a shorter neck.

**Below** A kerchief tied this way might have been smart in the nineties, but then, as now, it disappears on Trinny.
**Right** With her longer neck, Trinny can wear a thick scarf looped and tied.

# BELTS

It's all a question of position and width with belts. We are no longer expected to wear leather belts in the day, leaving the fancy ones for night. Anything goes at any time, especially when the belt concerned is worn with jeans. There is no point in even considering a belt before you have worked out the ideal place for your waistline. That is, does your pot belly require a waistband that cuts across it or is your bottom

## skinny little belt!

so large it needs to be halved by a hipster waistband?

Width of belt and buckle size can make a difference to a belt looking cool or not. Wearing a belt that hits a dodgy part of your torso will double the deformity by drawing attention to it.

# BELTS

A few hints on belts.

• If you are small boned, keep the buckle small or delicate, even if you're overweight.

• Those with dinosaur bones can go for bust with bold, big, chunky buckles.

• But they don't look great in thin belts, even if they are super-skinny.

• When you are wearing one colour head to toe, don't break it up with a different coloured belt.

**Below left** A waisted belt only emphasises and enlarges Trinny's bottom half.
**Below** Trinny looks best in a bold belt with a large buckle that rests on her hips.

• You can wear funky buckles with everything as long as you keep the belt monochrome.

• Big boobs don't look great with big belts, because it all becomes too complicated.

• Short waists, too, must beware of wide belts because they eat up what waist you do have, giving the illusion that your tits hang low enough to touch your middle.

• Long backs must wear belts low to stop their bum looking too big from the back.

**Below left** The same big buckle does no favours for Susannah, especially when it's at waist level.
**Below** A slightly smaller buckle with the belt resting on her hips flatters Susannah's curvaceous shape.

# NECKLACES

Jesus, what a shocker Susannah's face is in that necklace. Even without the necklace it is a horrifying example of age catching up like a stealth bomber. One doesn't often see oneself from this angle and our first piece of advice is to avoid the side mirror view. It's forced Susannah into thinking it might be time for Botox.

**Left** Susannah's short neck should not be encased in a dog collar-style necklace, nor should non-matching earrings be competing with the necklace.

The beauty of necklaces is that they need not be heirlooms to lift an outfit from the bottom step of mediocrity to the highest echelons of a Best Dresser. Look at Audrey Hepburn in Breakfast at Tiffany's or Jackie O in The White House; they both understood the power of a plain dress teamed with a fabulous necklace.

**Below** Susannah and Trinny in necklaces that are perfect for their body shape and size.

# NECKLACES

The bottom line is that if you have a short neck, squat face or big tits, or if you in any way are unfortunate enough to resemble Susannah, then necklaces should be one of the lesser items in your accessory collection. Unhappily short necks, especially necks with a suggestion of a double or triple chin, look terrible in necklaces.

• Long necks are easy to strangle because they look fab in chokers, chunky pieces and long, dangly jewelled wreaths. They are genetically bred to wear necklaces, although even they have their limitations.

• Look at the neckline of your top as well as the tone of your outfit before deciding which beaded collar to wear. Slash neck styles are barred from necklaces...do earrings instead.

• Big tits cannot do long and dangly because the line of the necklace becomes distorted once it hits the chest.

• Short necks are best entwined by delicate pieces that don't take up too much space between the chin and the breasts.

• Sloping, padded-with-fat shoulders are best suited to necklaces that are fine and filamented

**Above** Susannah's short neck and big tits compete for attention with this chunky necklace.

with small beads; angular, architectural necklaces need a good pair of coat-hanger shoulders to carry them off.

• Flat chests are wonderful boards on which to rest a huge show-stopping piece that can reach as low as your tummy button.

• Never wear lots of gold chains together unless you are a rap star.

• As you will only be wearing a polo neck with FLAT BOOBS, a long necklace that is bold and flamboyant is the S & T approved option. Chains and pendants over polo necks look cheap.

• Long necks look weak and giraffe-like when circled by a thin choker. They can carry something much wider and look amazing in it.

• A long neck coming out of a round neck top looks fabulous with a big chunky necklace at collarbone level.

• Don't wear an over-the-top-necklace and wild earrings together unless they are part of a set.

• Big boobs can carry off a delicate droplet necklace that ends just at the top of the cleavage. Never allow a pendant to disappear into a cleavage ravine.

**Above** The right necklace for Susannah is is delicate, thus extending the length of her neck and not competing with other features.

'It's what you leave off a dress, that makes it smart'

**Nettie Rosenstein**

On the contrary,
clever use of a
decorative touch can
transform a cheap-
looking outfit into an
expensive-looking one.

S

# EARRINGS

How can anyone create fashion frisson with a pair of earrings? Surely these are the one accessory immune to style flu? Unfortunately we know otherwise. Bad earring-wearing habits appear to be spreading all over the country. Wide gold hoops engraved with fancy twirly lines worn next to a gold sleeper, next to a stud, is very popular, very pedestrian and very ugly. Pearl studs are fab worn with ultra lady-like clothes, but become uninspiring and dull when worn all the time.

Amazingly the shape of one's face, the length of the neck and how many chins you own have a huge impact on the shape of earrings that are right for you. You'd expect your hairstyle to be important too, but it's not. Same with clothing. Obviously mega-diamonds with wellies and mac is odd (unless you're naked underneath), but generally the more unexpected the pairing the better it looks.

• Long faces look good in chandelier-shaped earrings and they're able to carry off a stud.

what are those?

- Round and dangly earrings will make a fatter face and chin look thinner.
- Round faces and hanging chins should stay away from studs or circular clip-ons.
- Short necks become even shorter next to long, dangly earrings that hang to the shoulder.
- If a short neck or small face wants to do discreet, opt for a plain gold or silver sleepers rather than studs.
- Plain golf-ball-sized hoops suit everyone.
- If the colours of your earrings complement your outfit they can be as sparkly as you like, even for the day.
- Cool earrings can transform a plain Jane.
- Don't wear fancy, dangly earrings if you want to look professional and relatively serious. Better to go for a great bracelet, brooch or necklace.
- Diamante looks wonderful when it is full on, over the top, but not so hot as when it's trying to be diamond stud. The latter looks like something fake trying to be real whereas a chandelier earring celebrates its false origins.

# RINGS

A ring is the most symbolic of all
jewellery pieces. It is a sign of love,
a token of commitment, a public display
of personal heritage. It signifies hieratical
positioning in the Catholic Church and gratitude
from the father to mother for the safe birth of
their child. They can also be bloody good fun,
as fake as you wish and worn with glee on any
finger you like (except the thumb, unless you
are Phoebe from Friends).

If you have small-boned fingers, you are
unable to take anything too bold. Your partner
or prospective fiancé will be thrilled that his
diamond doesn't have to compete with that

of Elizabeth Taylor. You, on the other hand, will be
gutted that your finger will not be sporting a stone
the size of an ice rink.

There is an upside, however, because your
fingers are beautifully suited to more delicate
antique pieces that involve much more
craftsmanship and thoughtful design.

The chances are your ring will be more original than that of dear Lizzie.

If your knuckles and joints could black out Lennox Lewis without gloves in the first round, you can think big. Your true love will have to compete with Richard Burton, and size, in this instance, matters.

The upside here is that your fingers can carry off wonderful costume jewellery that may cost next to nothing but still be real dazzlers. Large hands look a little more fragile when burdened by a big ring.

Nowadays any stone goes at any time of day, but too many rings on a finger detract from their individual beauty, and a ring on every finger is exceptionally tacky. One stunner is better than eight mediocre bands.

**Opposite top and bottom** A dainty band is lost on a big-boned hand whereas this pretty costume piece looks fabulous. **This page top and bottom** Women with small nails and fine bones should avoid the knuckle-duster look. They suit more finely wrought rings.

# BRACELETS

A bracelet is a great present for yourself or for a girlfriend. If it's someone you loathe, but are obliged to give to, like a hateful sister-in-law, just buy her the wrong shape. She will be delighted. The subtlety of its inappropriateness will be lost on her.

Bracelets are the only piece of jewellery that can look great en masse. It doesn't look cheap to have 20 bangles on your arm, just as long as they are all from the same family. Think of an Indian lady, beautiful in her sari, her arms ringed by scores of thin gold bangles; they look wonderful. Then think of an arm dripping with clunky gold charm bracelets, various-sized chains and the odd bangle, and the image isn't quite so pleasing.

**Left** Trinny, having a larger bone structure, can wear a chunky bracelet; the diamanté bracelet is lost on her arm.

**Opposite** On Susannah, the heavier bracelet makes her arm look chubby, while a more delicate style gives a slim and elegant look.

Unless gold and silver is in the same bracelet as a design feature, don't put these two metals together. They try to outshine each other and end up looking lacklustre.

• You've guessed it: small bones are better off with delicate bracelets whereas bigger wrists are able to carry off something much chunkier.

• Wearing two identical cuffs on each arm is a sophisticated method of achieving instant style.

• Buy lots of the same cheap bracelet and wear them all together for a lush look.

• A bracelet worn with a watch can be pretty as long as it doesn't overpower the timepiece and looks like it never need come off.

• Secondhand and charity shops are brilliant foraging grounds for retro pieces.

# SHOES THICK ANKLES FLAT

For those with thick ankles, flat shoes with a thin toe make the ankle look even stumpier. A high ankle strap strangles the ankle, and a low kitten heel is in danger of looking like it's going to snap under your weight.

A more substantial shoe looks in proportion to a more substantial ankle so a chunky loafer is a good choice. A simple thong lends much-needed length to a thick ankle, and clogs are a thick ankle's best friend.

These shoes would make thick ankles look truly titanic.

Shoes to turn a a shapeless ankles into a respectable part of the body

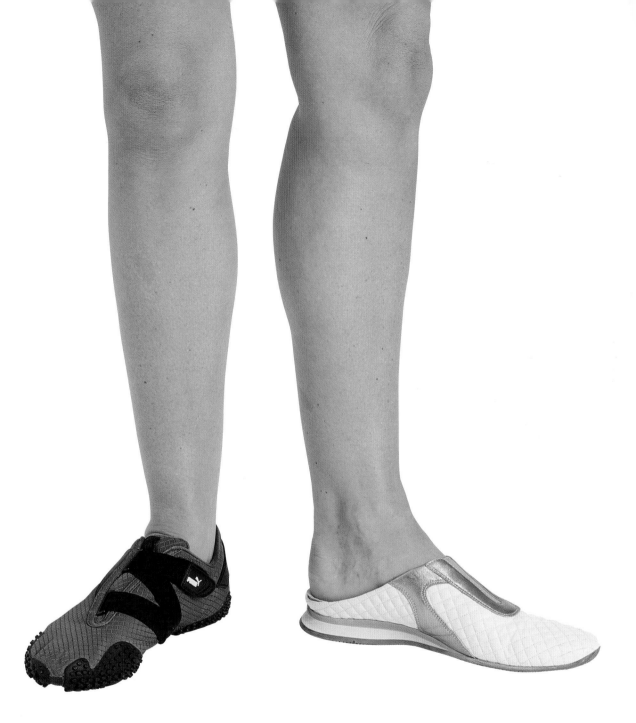

A full trainer will make the leg look short and stubby.

A flat mule elongates the leg, giving the appearance of a thin ankle.

Those with thick ankles will find that a heeled shoe with a high back cuts into and covers up the thinnest part of the ankle so making matters worse. Slingbacks with kitten heels and mules with a thin heel will both look like you have squashed a large leg into a tiny shoe.

If you wear a court shoe, make sure the heel comes straight down from the base of the shoe which will give your ankle some shape. A slingback can look good with a high sturdy heel and a heavy heel on a wedge mule will make your ankles appear thinner.

Delicate heels exaggerate a thick ankle.

These styles flatter and distract attention from your ankles.

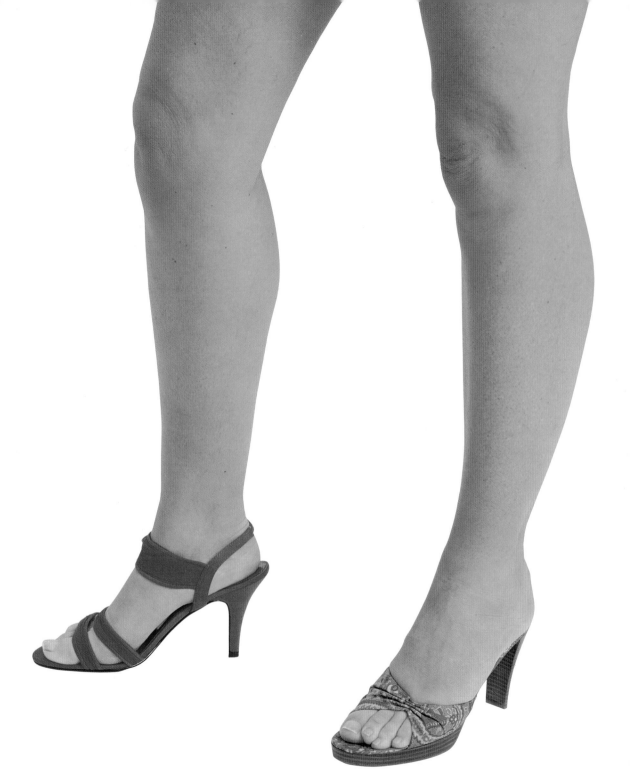

The ankle strap cuts off the length of the foot and takes the eye to the least flattering part of the leg.

The low cut of this shoe draws the eye down and away from the ankle.

# SHOES THIN ANKLES FLAT

Thin ankles will look like trees stuck in concrete in clumpy shoes such as Birkenstock clogs. Even a ballet pump will appear to swamp the foot, and large details, such as flowers, tend to overpower a thin ankle.

If you wear an open-backed shoe it needs to be a thong sandal so the flow of your leg isn't broken. Pointed toes finish off the ankle in a less jarring way than a round toe. Any detail in the front of the shoe should be delicate.

These shoes will only emphasise a skinny ankle and leg.

But these styles help sylph-like ankles look their best.

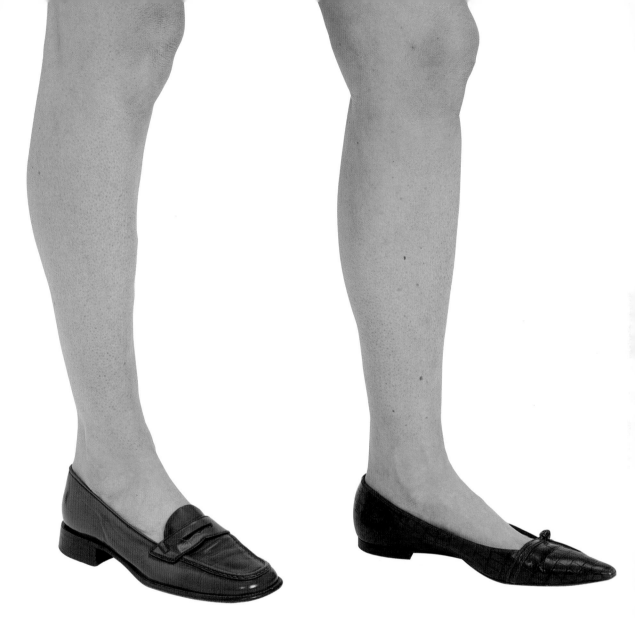

The high front and chunky heel of this style of shoe are too heavy for a delicate ankle.

A pointed toe with a slim heel will flatter the leg.

# SHOES THIN ANKLES HEELS

Beware of hefty heels if you are blessed with thin ankles. They dominate the shoe, make your feet look enormous and exaggerate the skinniness of your ankles.

More elegant heels will allow the wearer to show off her ankles to best advantage without the shoes detracting from them and drawing too much attention to her feet.

If your ankles are dainty, shoes like these will make your feet look enormous.

The shoe styles above are much more flattering for a slender ankle.

When wearing ankle straps, the usual rules apply – a slender heel is much more flattering to a thin ankle than a chunky heel.

# BOOTS

We work with countless numbers of women who shy away from skirts because they are ashamed of their legs.

We say: 'That's why boots were invented.'

They say: 'My calves are too big and I can't get a boot on.'

We reply: 'Have you tried the pull-on version?'

They haven't.

We say: 'You'll get them over your legs and they will be your passport to ever-after skirt wearing.'

They give it a go and suddenly a new world of dressing opens up.

If you have ankles that really should be hidden, the boot allows you to wear skirts of all lengths. Boots have saved thousands of women from a lifetime in trousers. This doesn't mean, however, that dainty legs are privileged in being able to wear every type of boot. They can't, and a thin calf can look just as dodgy in the wrong boot as a thick one does in a skirt.

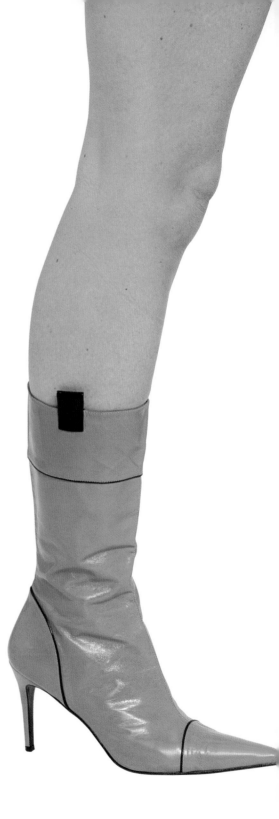

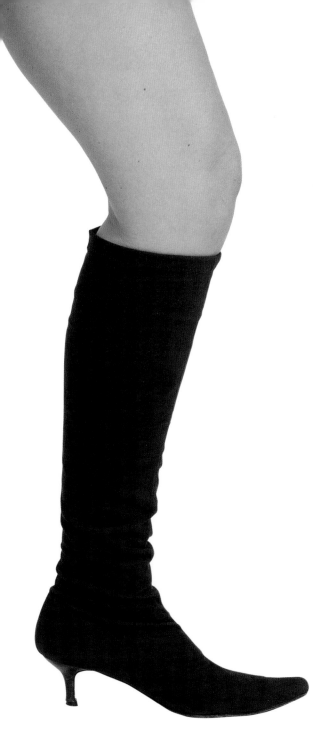

- **Thin legs can look like sticks in pull-on boots if they are too loose around the calf.**
- **Big boobs need a thicker heel on their boot to balance the body shape.**
- **Try to avoid having a gap between the top of your boot and your skirt.**
- **If you do, fill it with fun tights, like fishnets.**
- **Don't tuck your trousers into a pair of ankle boots. You'll look like a pantomime character.**
- **If zip-ups just won't zip up your chunky calf, buy pull-ons. They will seem to take inches off your ankles.**
- **Thin legs look great in heel-free boots; fat legs don't.**

**Opposite** If you are cursed with chunky calves, calf-length boots will only emphasise your problem.
**Left** Finding a boot that totally encases your lower leg is the best way to distract attention from chunky calves.

'Accessories can make or break an outfit. Apart from a few exceptions it is better to tone rather than match exactly.'

# 07
# Storage

When Trinny is in a foul mood Susannah can guarantee her wardrobe has been hit by a tornado. A relaxed and composed Trinny springs from beautifully re-arranged shelves (again) that look like something only Mother Nature could create with such precision.

Extraordinary, don't you think, that a tidy wardrobe can have such an effect. Susannah always laughed at her partner's anal-retentiveness. 'I mean, how utterly puerile. The girl is spitting hatpins because her wardrobe is a bit untidy. She should see mine!'

The fact of the matter was that Susannah was reduced to a pulp of quivering frustration every morning because her outfit searching was like beating a path through virgin rain forest. Her life was severely hampered and compromised because she was too sodding lazy to order her clothes. A big day meant finding and trying on endless clothes the night before the event. The consequence of which was less story time for the kids or an enraged husband yelling at her to get a move on.

There will no doubt be many of you who identify with Susannah. Your wardrobes will be bursting at the seams but there is nothing to wear. When you are running late all your decent clothes cower at the back of the cupboard. Trousers huddle in one corner, shirts in another. Jackets hide under coats. You negotiate with what you can find then beg them to look fabulous. They never do.

A life-changing event such as a new baby makes the situation even worse as your house is overtaken by tiny clothes and toys. It's imperative to order your storage space is well ordered if you don't want to spend the rest of your life in chaos.

If your wardrobe is a mess you assume you are bereft of things you actually have. You go shopping. Spend more money. Then find its twin back in the wardrobe. It was there all the time. This is when you think, 'Okay, I'd better have a tidy up.' A swift swipe of organisation and you think you have changed the world. The wardrobe looks neater, yes. But its contents remain a mystery. Why? Well, nothing has been hung or put away with an ounce of intelligence.

You need a brain to tidy clothes? No. But the method of Trinny's madness you do need. It sounds crazy, but perfectly displayed clothing will have a huge impact on your day and save you loads of time, especially if you store winter clothes elsewhere in the summer.

Less to choose from also makes for sharper decision-making. What's the point of having lovely clothes that suit your body shape if you don't have time to put them together or can't find them. Ordered shelves also start the day with clarity. There is nothing worse than the morning madness of riffling through bits of material that you don't recognise because they are so crumpled. It's more than depressing.

When sorting your clothes in an efficient way it has to be done with forethought and planning. It's not just a question of taking things off wire hangers and putting them on plastic ones. You need to invest in tidiness by buying padded and clip hangers that will make your clothing look beautiful and last longer. The easier it is to see the entire contents of your wardrobe, the easier it is to choose an outfit.

Something so small can waste as much time as the inability to pull together an outfit. Don't just think about the clothes you are wearing; it's the accessories too that need to be regimented.

Susannah was unable or perhaps unwilling to turn the corner called intelligent storage, so it took intervention from her friend. The results since that day have been amazing. Thanks to Trinny's help, Susannah is no longer late and her kids benefit from an entire story at night as opposed to just one chapter.

# UNDERWEAR

Organising your bras, knickers, tights and socks does require some effort, but it's the base on which to build an outfit, and it will save valuable time in the early morning rush hour.

Start by lining your drawers with pretty paper or splurge out and buy cardboard or plastic dividers. You can even use old shoe boxes. And invest in some lavender bags for a good smell.

Then divide your bras and knickers into style and colour – everyday, evening and sport.

Keep tights, hold-ups and stockings separately from socks. And separate dark-coloured tights and stockings so you don't confuse them in poor light. Don't put back any that have runs or holes. Socks can be put into categories for style and warmth – cotton, wool, cashmere, walking and sport.

Once you've made the effort to sort everything out, keep it tidy. We never seem to have enough drawer or wardrobe space so finding imaginative methods of storage for all items of clothing is of major importance. The golden rule is never to store anything that is dirty.

Giving the layout of your wardrobe a thorough going over is almost as therapeutic as a shopping spree. You will meet old friends and team them up in new and imaginative ways.

If you don't have much space available, store out-of-season clothes and shoes in suitcases under the bed. It's worth the effort and a good chance for a seasonal cull.

# JEWELLERY

Necklaces and bracelets can be hung on wardrobe doors instead of hidden away in boxes where they are hard to find and easy to forget about. They'll look good and seeing them will remind you to wear them more often.

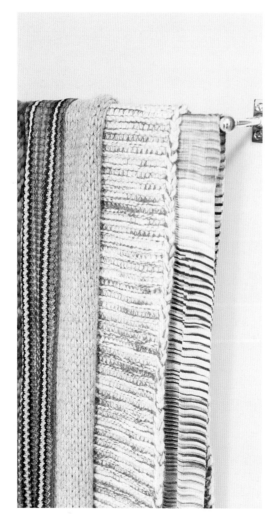

# SCARVES

Trinny keeps her scarves folded over a tie rack on the doors of the wardrobe where she stores her tops and jerseys – again, this means she will remember to wear them. They are divided into wool, cashmere and silk.

Scarves can also be folded neatly in small piles according to fabric so you can see the colours easily.

Hats can be stored inside each other in hat boxes with a separating layer of newspaper between each hat.

Belts can be hung together on tie racks or each one placed over the hook of a hanger with the outfit you wear it with.

# FOLDING

The perfectionist that she is, Trinny stores all her T shirts, sweats and jerseys in gradations of colour, in piles that are not too high and leaving a reasonable space in between each pile. Keep the piles narrow for good visibility, neatness and easy access.

Don't put away a jersey or T shirt that is dirty. Wash it immediately or take it to the dry cleaners – moths love food-encrusted clothes, and most especially wool and cashmere.

Heavy jumpers can be put away for the summer months – after being hand washed or dry cleaned, then folded in plastic bags. Old dry cleaning covers are ideal for this.

Jeans can be folded and stored on shelves as it doesn't matter if they are a little crushed, in fact they should be.

Scatter your shelves with fragrant cinnamon sticks, cloves or lavender bags to help keep moths at bay.

# HANGING

Hanging clothes in an ordered way is the secret to making the most of your wardrobe. We hang as many clothes as we can because it's easier than folding and it's certainly easier to see what you have to hand.

You will need decent hangers – preferably padded, wooden or plastic – for dresses and tops, and clip hangers for trousers and skirts. Hang coats and jackets on wooden hangers.

Banish wire hangers entirely – they cause creasing and unsightly bulges on the shoulders.

When you hang clothes, try to create outfits or group them in colours which go together. Hang camisoles next to cardigans, tops next to a skirt or trousers of a complementary colour. Trinny changes the hanging order of her clothes on a regular basis, and always finds an unthought-of match.

Hang trousers from the hem – it will save on ironing.

Put lavender bags on the hangers for a special touch.

'Chaos is a friend of mine'

Bob Dylan

And, boy, does it show.

# FOOTWEAR

This part of the wardrobe invariably looks a mess. If you have the space, the ideal solution is the shoe rack cupboard. If you don't have the luxury of sufficient space, shoes should be stored in their boxes where they won't gather dust or get lost under a pile of their peers. Attach a polaroid or a photograph to the box for easy identification.

You will need a good cleaning kit and shoe trees to hold the shape. Cedar trees are good for shoes that are inclined to smell; plastic shoe trees are fine for most other shoes.

On the subject of smell: keep shoes that tend to smell and trainers separately. If your shoes get wet, stuff them with newspaper and keep in a cool dry place until they are completely dry.

It's a good idea to alternate shoes rather than wear the same pair day after day. They will last a lot longer. And keep them well polished – they look better and the polish will help to repel water.

'

**It took Susannah ten years to learn from Trinny the benefits of a more anally organised wardrobe. As a result, she feels as if she has more clothes and can spend more time doing other things she knows are important. '**

# 08 Beauty

Are you a beauty believer or not? Do you have faith that those giant cosmetic conglomerates have your blackheads, cellulite and flaky elbows in mind each time they launch a new product with a multi-million dollar marketing spend? Do they want nothing more than to see you with a clear complexion or the softest skin? Do Uma Thurman and Elizabeth Hurley really care about your beauty issues? And do they, as beauty figureheads, actually use the products they endorse?

Are you in need of a change in your beauty routine? If you are a women in a midlife crisis, a good way to start this new phase of your life is to chuck out all the old creams and potions you have used since you were 16 and begin again. What suited your flawless teenage face will not work against the onslaught of wrinkles and weather-worn blemishes.

It's very easy to be cynical about the wonders of face creams enriched with baby lamb embryos or a series of alphabetical and numerical formulas that are designed to make you think a science of some sort has been involved in making this or that product unique. Heavily touched-up photography in the pages of all the glossy magazines and the billions of predominantly US dollars made by these businesses only add to our scepticism about the beauty industry and what it claims it can do.

Anything promising you a miracle cure or an instant transformation is seriously pulling the surgical gauze over your eyes. Those purporting to give a face-lift in a pot know full well that the only thing able to iron out wrinkles is a scalpel, hard tugs and stitches. Anything that has the word 'firming' in its sales pitch needs to be used with a pinch of salt.

That said, there are many products that do what they say, and yes, we know for a fact that Elizabeth Hurley has no desire to use anything other than Estée Lauder. The key to beauty buying, aside from heading a campaign or having a PhD in chemistry, is to keep your expectations low and allow time for the magic formulas to work.

Now when it comes to shelling out on beauty products there is no limit to what's out there. You can spend hundreds of pounds on a single cream only to find the same results in something much cheaper. It's easy to make costly mistakes, like buying creams that are too rich for your age or too oily for the ever-lurking spots.

So in this chapter we have highlighted certain products and also divided most of them into three categories. One for those who are prepared for the long-term view – and are filthy rich or vain beyond belief. One for those who want to help their looks along without spending huge amounts of time and having to forfeit the kitchen extension this year. And one for those who want a short-term fix that's cheap, or better still, absolutely free.

There is nothing like a good scrubbing with domestic salt (beware the open wounds) to make you feel fantastic. The home remedies that we have devised over the years have spawned from desperation when we've been bereft of any beauty help. A toothbrush to plump up lips, toothpaste (or vodka) for spots and haemorrhoid cream for under-eye bags may seem totally mad to you, but believe us…they work.

Some of you may remain sceptical even after reading this practical and realistic take on beauty. Susannah was the same. A hardcore non-believer. But as she has got older, the importance of body maintenance – as with a tired old van – has never been more evident.

There won't be any overnight transformations, but a little help from selected friends in a bottle will make you feel that you are more in control of the ageing process.

# SPOTS

If you don't have to read this section, how lucky you are. Trinny envies you. But the bottom line is that most women have spots at some time or another.

Trinny suffered from years of acne before she discovered her long-term solution. If you suffer like she did, you too might be looking for help. For others, with spots caused by stress, periods or over-eating of chocolate, there are easier ways of dealing with the problem. Although dermatologists will tell you that spots have little to do with what you eat, how many of you have had a chocolate binge only to discover a couple of unwanted red throbbers the next day?

Toothpaste can be a great emergency fixer as it will dry out the spot. Just make sure you are sleeping alone that night or your partner has already started snoring.

Drinking lots of water will flush out toxins and does help your skin. There are also great products out there that contain salacylic acid. Eve Lom's Dynaspot is one example.

Good concealers can totally cover up the problem. (Look at Laura Mercier's Secret Camouflage in the Make-up chapter.) Just remember, we have nearly all been there and if you don't want lasting memories of those spots on your face, DON'T PICK. You will regret it.

**For spot control**, toothpaste, any brand, is always to hand.

## Short term

Colgate fluoride toothpaste
ESPA Essential Tea Tree Gel
Eve Lom Dynaspot
The Organic Pharmacy Spot Gel
Origins Spot Remover
Tisserand Tea-Tree & Kanuka Blemish Stick

## Medium term

Dr Hauschka
Inner Cosmetic Capsules
Elizabeth Kompala's
Problem Skin Lotion
Jan Marini Bioglycolic Bioclear Cream
Mudd Mask
The Organic Pharmacy Complete Acne Kit: contains external preparations and internal supplements for a holistic approach
Peter Thomas Roth AHA/BHA Acne Clearing Gel

## Long term

Roaccutane: a very strong prescription-only medicine for long-term acne – cured Trinny's. Can have side effects so use only under medical supervision

# SUN

As teenagers, neither Susannah nor Trinny felt any guilt about using olive oil on a bed of tinfoil to change their lily-white complexions to something akin to a horse's saddle. But now they have realised the importance of sunblock and the effects of sun damage on the skin.

The safest option for a golden glow is a fake tan, but if you are in the sun, remember to apply sunblock on every exposed part of your body. Skin cancers are often found in overlooked areas, such as the soles of the feet and ankles. Dark and black skin needs equal protection.

The bottom line is that sun protection should be worn every day in order to avoid long-term sun damage – there are great daily moisturisers with a SPF of 15+. If you already suffer from sun damage, there are solutions. The best are for the pigmentation that can develop over the years, especially among pregnant women. Some of these products contain strong ingredients, so if you use them and want to go in the sun soon afterwards, wear very high factor protection – or your problem will return with a vengence.

**St Tropez** Whipped Bronze self-tanning system.

## Fake tanning

Boots Soltan Easitan

Clarins Auto-Bronzant range

Clarins After Sun Shimmer Oil

Dr Hauschka Toned Day Cream

Fantasy Tan: the original airbrush tan applied by a beauty consultant

Jan Marini Bioglycolic Sunless Self-tanner

Jean-Paul Mist-On Tan: spray tan, available at Heidi Klein

Lancaster Self-tan range

Model Co's Tan Airbrush in a Can: do it in the shower!

Phytomer Bronzinstant

St Tropez self-tanning system

Vichy Auto Bronzant

## Sun protection

Oenobiol Solaire: a supplement that helps your body prepare for tanning

Clarins Sun Protection range

Dr Hauschka Sun Care range (mineral only)

Esthederm Sea & Tropics Sun Tan Lotion, available at Space NK

Garnier Ambre Solaire Sheer Protect SPF30

Jan Marini Daily Face Protectant SPF30

Lancaster Sun Care range

Origins Out Smart Face Protector SPF25

Riemann P20 Once-a-day SunFilter

## Sun damage/age spots

Barefoot Botanicals Rosa Fina Intensive Facial Radiance Cream

Dr Sebagh Pure Vitamin C Powder Cream

Environ Intensive range

Futur-Tec Aged Hands Treatment

Helena Rubenstein Life Pearl

Jan Marini Even-Tone Pigment Lightening Gel

Jan Marini Glycolic Acid Peel

Korner Prove Real Serum

Korner Look Famous Purifying Mask

Aurora Photo-rejuvenation Intense Pulsed Light treatment from The French Cosmetic Medical Company; IPL treatments are also available at good aestheticians and cosmetic clinics

# CELLULITE

It's fat. Nothing else. Your long-term enemy that just doesn't budge. Desperate for the ultimate cure, we all read the magazine articles. It's not there yet, but certain treatments help.

Let's start with the diet. It's a documented fact that certain foods and drinks will aid and abet the development of cellulite. Avoid all caffeine, fizzy drinks, buttery croissants and pastry, and drink, drink, drink, water, water, water, flush, flush, flush.

Good circulation is the enemy of cellulite, so first thing in the morning when your body is sluggish, before you have a shower, wake it up with a body brush. From your fingers and toes to your heart, brush in one direction waking up your circulation along the way. Get in the shower, and if you can bear it, switch from hot to cold water to continue the process. Once in the shower, slap on one of the body scrub products that contain menthol to stimulate the nerve endings or seaweed to detox the system.

After the shower, yet more products are available that continue the process (Trinny rates Thalgo). The success of this system depends on your discipline to continue doing it daily.

If you are a bit lazy, and not too strapped for cash, go for a treatment like Endermologie or Mesotherapy. These are more penetrating than anything you can do at home.

**The first step,** the body brush and water.

## Short term

Barefoot Botanicals Rosa Fina Body Conditioning Lotion

Decléor Contour Slimming Range

Phytomer Body Declic Contouring Range

Rodial Body Sculpture

Rodial 3 in 1 Body Scrub

Sisley Phyto-sculpt

Global Anti Cellulite

Thalgo Thalgomince Range

Thalgo Thalgogive Refining Serum

Thalgo Spray Frigimince

## Medium term

Avoid fizzy drinks, coffee, tea and croissants

Drink plenty of water

ESPA Detoxifying Seaweed Bath

Skin brushing with medium-bristle brush such as Riffi massagebüret or ESPA skin brush

Origins Let's Circulate Salt Rub Soap

Phytomer Body Declic Anti Cellulite Cream

Oenobiol Aquadrainant: nutritional supplement to help with water retention which contributes to cellulite

## Long term

Regular massage, available from Dr Hauschka trained aestheticians; Nari Sadhuram; Perfectly at Home; D-Stress or contact your local alternative therapy clinic

Lymphatic drainage massage: Fiona & Marie Aesthetics, Bliss

Endermologie treatment: works on localised fat and water retention and boosts circulation. Also tones, firms and smoothes the skin, giving a more refined figure

Eporex Cellulite Mesotherapy treatment: the mesotherapy ingredients stimulate body processes which detoxify, increase the burning of fat and improve circulation

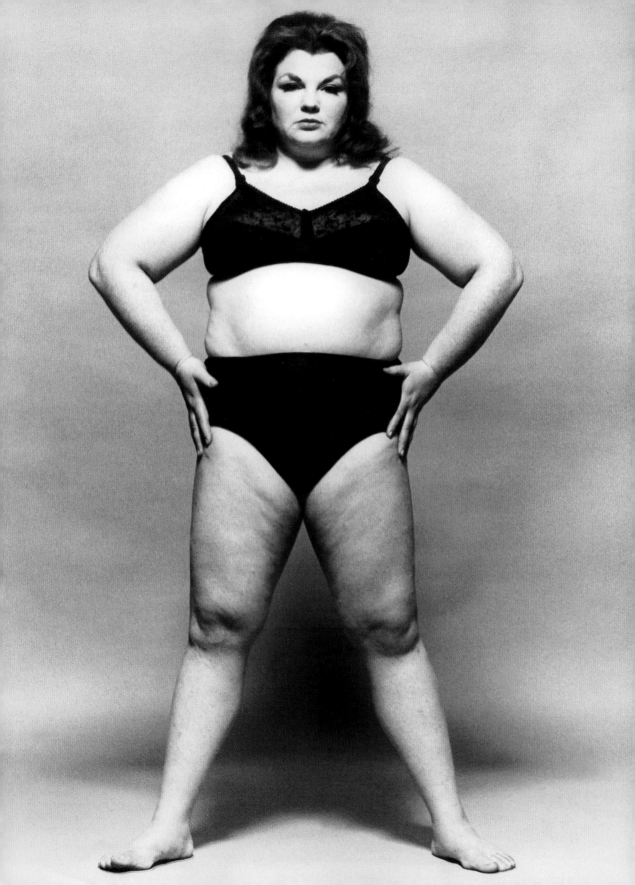

# HAIR REMOVAL

There is nothing more unsightly than a hairy leg (well, maybe a hairy bottom). It's really a question of how you choose to tackle it. The question of how to get rid of superfluous body hair has vexed the beauty industry since time began, starting with the Middle Eastern technique of sugaring to the latest light therapies. The choice is yours.

The quickest hair removal for legs is still the razor, but it is also the least long lasting. Buy your own razor – there is no quicker route to a blood-spotted shin than using your partner's cast-off Bic disposable.

There is no denying the moment of pain, but waxing will give you the smoothest hair-free legs. Whether you attempt this at home using a strip kit or opt for the more effective hot wax salon treatment, both will take longer to show hair regrowth than the razor.

For the ultimate fix there are Intense Pulsed Light therapies. These are particularly effective for smaller areas where you may find that hair is really unsightly (such as face and bikini line), but you will need several visits in order to treat a full cycle of hair growth. This treatment is progressive, so the more you have it the weaker the hair follicle becomes. Successful treatments have resulted in a permanently hair-free area.

**The quickest solution:** a razor.

## Short term

Gillette Venus Razor
Nair Glide-on Hair Remover

## Medium term

Rica Azulene Lipowax
with Beauty Tools wax heater

Wax A Way: waxing hair removal system

## Long term

Aurora Intense Pulsed Light Hair Removal from The French Cosmetic Medical Company; IPL treatments are also available at good aestheticians and cosmetic clinics

'Becoming the new feminine ideal requires just the right combination of insecurity, exercise, bulimia and surgery'

Gary Trudeau

**Oh, so the ideal woman is worn out, clone-like and in therapy for an eating disorder?**

**s**

# SMALL BOOBS

Even if you are usually happy with the size of your boobs, there are times when a slightly enhanced shape is just the ticket. Sometimes a little shading in the cleavage to contour the breasts is enough to make a dress work, but this is most successful coupled with a gel-filled bra. For the most convincing cleavage, combine the Wonderbra with chicken fillet silicone inserts and a brush of contouring powder.

If you don't want to put your tits away in your sock drawer at the end of the evening, it may be worth investigating the latest wonder of science, the Brava bra. This vacuum pump machine sucks at your breasts for 10 hours a day for 10 weeks, at the end of which it is claimed that they will have grown a cup size!

The final solution is surgery. There are more new techniques being developed daily – which one is right for you? We've heard (and seen!) all the horror stories, but the truth is that many women feel happier and more self-confident after breast augmentation. Before you make any decision, do your research, read the magazines, ask friends who you trust. Read the Beauty Lowdowns series of books by Wendy Lewis. If you're still unsure, you can have a consultation with Wendy either by telephone or in person. Take your time and make sure that you're entirely confident before going ahead.

The Brava bra.

## Short term

Clever shading with make-up
Myla cleavage-enhancer bra implants
Ultimo Gel-filled bras
Wonderbra

## Medium term

Brava bra

## Long term

Breast augmentation surgery: before you make any decision to have plastic surgery, do your research and make sure that you know exactly what you are letting yourself in for

# LIPS

Up until a few years ago, what God gave you in the lips department was with you for life. But with the introduction of collagen and hyaluronic acid (babies are full of this and look at their skin), thin lips are a thing of the past.

If your problem is simply dry lips, slap on some lip balm. For thin lips, try Susannah's trick of brushing a damp toothbrush back and forth

**A toothbrush** is a useful and quick way of livening up lips.

over the lips (not too hard) for a minute. Lip plumpers will make thin lips temporarily fatter. DuWop's Lip Venom contains cinnamon, which reacts on your lips and makes them tingle.

For those with lined lips (either through smoking or talking too much), the best medium-term solution is to use a wax-based product around the lined area to fill in the cracks. Trinny also massages her wrinkle cream into her lips every night for two minutes.

If you are looking for a long-term solution for either lip plumping or just line filling, make sure, before you succumb to the likes of Restylane (a hyaluronic acid filler) or Hylaform, that you work out how much bigger you really want your lips. The technician who does the treatment should be able to work out the best lip size to suit your features. There are new fillers coming on to the market all the time, so check with your technician that the one you choose has undergone sufficiently rigorous research.

## Short term

Aveda Lip Saver SPF 15
Crème de la Mer The Lip Balm
DuWop Lip Venom
Dr Hauschka Lip Balm
Helena Rubenstein
Collagenist Lip Zoom
NV Perricone ALA Lip Plumper

## Medium term

Mary Cohr New Youth Lip Care
Origins Line Chaser
Paula Dorf Line Smoother
The Organic Pharmacy
Lip & Eye Treatment Cream
Prescriptives Magic range Invisible
Line Smoother
Scrub your lips gently
with a soft toothbrush each night

## Long term

Hyaluronic acid filler such as
Restylane Touch, Hylaform or
Juvaderm from Fiona & Marie
Aesthetics, Dr Sebagh and all
good cosmetic surgeons and facial
aestheticians

# EYES

There is no part of the face that will benefit more from a good night's sleep than the eye area; eyes really are the barometer for the rest of the face. But if a good night's sleep is not forthcoming and you wake up feeling the worse for wear, there are products, such as Dr Hauschka Eye Solace Ampoules and Eyesential, that will give temporary relief and the feeling that your eyes have taken a stimulating shower.

For a daily fix, look at products from Givenchy, La Prairie and Jan Marini, which have really revolutionised the market. Although none of these products will bring long-lasting change to the actual eye area, we do believe that daily use will keep the age process slightly at bay. At the very least your make-up will apply better.

Botox is a solution for those who cannot abide the fact that the wrinkles under their eyes are going to meet their smile lines. A few pricks with a needle above the cheekbones freezes those lines from moving further south.

For those of us with suitcases under the eyes there is blepharoplasty – plastic surgery to remove the excess fat that builds up over the years. Dark circles can be helped by injecting hyaluronic acid underneath the cheekbones to raise them closer to the eyes and reduce dark circles  – Dr Sebagh developed this technique.

**Givenchy No Surgetics** – a medium-term fix for your eyes.

## Short term

Dr Hauschka Eye Solace Ampoules
Eyesential
Gatineau Collagen Compresses
Mark Traynor's Face and Neck Lift available from Screen Face
Origins No Puffery: cooling mask for eyes
Talika Eye Therapy Patch

## Medium term

Crème de la Mer The Eye Balm
Frownies
Givenchy No Surgetics eye range
Jan Marini Transformation Eye Cream
La Prairie Cellular Eye Moisturiser
NV Perricone ALA Eye Area Therapy & Vitamin C-Esta Eye Area Therapy
The Organic Pharmacy Double Rose Herbal Eye Serum
Talika Lipocils: encourages growth of eyebrows and lashes

## Long term

Botox
Lift 6 Facial
Restylane Touch
Blepharoplasty (surgical eye-lift) – as always, we recommend seeking the advice of an objective expert such as Wendy Lewis before you proceed

# WRINKLES

What about all these fabulously expensive creams on the market – do they work? All we can say is that by law in the United Kingdom it is impossible to sell a cream that will make a permanent change to your face without a prescription. We know women who swear by this or that cream – it's up to you.

A great temporary solution can be what you eat. Nico Perricone, in his book The Wrinkle Cure, states that salmon (not smoked) and cantaloupe a day or two before a big event (eaten at every meal, mind you) works wonders. We've tried this and it does plump up the skin.

We can both vouch for water as a great de-wrinkler. Other temporary solutions include CACI, the non-surgical face-lift; Dr Sebagh's miraculous cheekbone-lifting technique (as we get older they slip down our faces); and various pulsed light therapies.

The most permanent solution – the eye, brow or full face-lift – is a drastic measure, and if you don't want to end up looking like dear Joan, make sure before you proceed that you have all the info and that this is really what you want.

**DDF Wrinkle Relax** helps in the medium term.

## Short term

Estée Lauder Idealist Micro-D Deep Thermal Refinisher

Mark Traynor's Face and Neck Lift

## Medium term

Aveda Firming Fluid

Barefoot Botanical Rosa Fina Intensive Facial Radiance Cream

Crème de la Mer The Face Serum

DDF Wrinkle Relax

Eve Lom The Cleanser

Givenchy No Surgetics range

Jan Marini C-Esta Serum

Korner Prove Real Serum

Lancaster 365 Cellular Elixir

NV Perricone ALA Face Firming Activator

The Organic Pharmacy Super Antioxidant range

Peter Thomas Roth Max Retinol Wrinkle Repair with SPF20

Thalgo Wrinkle Control

## Long term

Lift 6 facial (latest treatment from the CACI people)

Polaris Tissue Tightening treatment using radio frequency, from the French Cosmetic Medical Company; radio frequency treatments are also available at good aestheticians and cosmetic clinics

Surgical face-lift – before making a decision, talk to more than one surgeon and get them to show you loads of before and after photos. Never feel that there is a question you cannot ask. A face-lift is a huge step for any woman and will have results that will stay with you forever

# TEETH

When you give your teeth a quick pre-dinner clean, do it twice. It makes all the difference. A visit to the hygienist is the next best thing and, although painful (Trinny requires medication before a visit), it will clean them really well.

Bleaching trays are slightly complicated. They involve a mould being taken of your teeth and two weeks of wearing a rather unattractive contraption in your mouth at night.

Susannah instead opted for the laser therapy (at a Dentics outlet) – one hour of a sinister-looking contraption holding your mouth open extremely wide. Great results though. After both treatments, avoid teeth-staining food or drink.

If you have developed a rather squit set of teeth over the years, think about having veneers or bonding. In bonding, a plastic resin is applied to teeth and sculpted into shape. Veneers are more costly but longer lasting – an individually shaped porcelain shell is placed over a tooth to improve its colour and shape. Changing your mouth can be one of the most effective ways of changing your face. Just make sure you avoid a Ross moment!

**Pearl Drops** teeth whitener, a quick fix.

## Short term

Pearl Drops Daily Whitening Toothpolish

## Medium term

Laser Bleaching at Dentics, Brite Smile UK, Q Clinic

## Long term

Porcelain veneers

# NECK

There are so many women who spend a fortune on their face and totally forget about their neck. The neck gets a hard time of it anyway. We recline in bed, neck bent towards book, wrinkles forming as we read. In the sun we forget our neck when applying the sun lotion. It's only when it's too late that we discover the place with the most lines on our bodies is our NECK.

How many face-lifts have we seen where the neck was forgotten? The combination of 30 upstairs and 50 below is dreadful. Like the hands. If you are reading this book in your thirties, remember the earlier you start the better. Slap on that moisturiser, SPF 20, and try to read less in bed. If you have hit your forties and the sag is setting in, no neck cream will give you any permanent results (although Sisley and La Prairie will give you temporary relief).

If you can bear it, Botox can be injected into certain necks, but you have to have the right muscles or it can be quite dangerous. If done regularly this can prevent further damage.

For the most permanent change, liposuction can remove excess fat, and a face-lift can add to a chin, thereby giving some shape that will hide the worst of the neck.

**Sisley Neck Cream** helps in the short term.

## Short term

Korres Passion Flower Firming and Line Smoothing Neck Cream
La Prairie Neck Cream
RéVive Fermitif Neck Renewal Cream
Sisley Neck Cream

## Medium term

Botox

## Long term

Polaris Tissue Tightening treatment using radio frequency, from the French Cosmetic Medical Company; radio frequency treatments are also available at good aestheticians and cosmetic clinics
Surgical neck lift

'There are those
fortunate few who
are born with beautiful
skin and don't really
need to try.
The rest of us
need not despair
because there *is* an
answer to every
beauty dilemma out
there.'

09

Hair

How many of us are really happy with our hair? Is it your crowning glory or your bête noir?

Are you a mum so busy you don't give your hair a second thought? Do you have long hair because your husband says he loves it long (it reminds him of your best days), but you have no time to style it so it spends its life in a ponytail which does nothing for your face? Or are you the sporty gym or riding type who feels her natural fitness and bubbly personality will shine through hair scraped back into that most awful of hair accessories – the dreaded scrunchie?

Whatever stage of life you are at, be it a mother of toddlers or teenagers, pulling your hair out in the throes of a midlife crisis, or going grey during menopause, there is nothing that improves your outlook on life more dramatically than a new hairdo.

Most of us can remember the thrill of a good hairstyle but not many of us are sufficiently meticulous about maintaining it. It's easy not to notice a gradual decline over the years. And it's very easy not to notice that you are sticking religiously to a fab haircut you got several years ago, imposing the same regime on it (even though it might look like a topiary hedge) and using styling products that can't help once the cut has grown out.

It might equally be that you have never been given the right haircut. We have come across countless women who have a fringe to hide the wrinkles, even though it's the worst style for their shape of face. And half of these women don't even have enough wrinkles to make it worthwhile.

You might have spent years gradually going blonder and blonder and now have a helmet head of one-coloured hair which doesn't suit anyone.

So many women stay with a style or a colour that suited them when they felt their most alluring and beautiful.

But they are now in their forties or fifties, their face has started sagging, they know they are looking a little worn, but rely on their hair to feel a blush of youth that has now passed them by. All it's actually doing is adding a very unflattering aspect to the face and dragging it down even further. It's time for those spaniel ears to come off. It's time for a change. And this can be achieved in a number of ways.

Some women suit going grey (and can look even more chic as they mature); others find their hair resembles a bad nicotine stain. If you fall into this category, ask yourself why you aren't considering colouring your hair. Is it just because you have never done it or are you afraid you will resemble that advert for Grecian 2000? Are the memories of your grandmother's blue rinse just too strong?

Cast all these thoughts from your mind, get yourself to a hairdresser now, and get a new lease of life with some gentle colouring or a new cut, or both.

A good haircut is low maintenance and it will take years off you.

We have sought the expert advice of hairdresser Richard Ward at 162B Sloane Street, London SW1. Richard has transformed the women who have appeared on our television programmes for several years now. For our book he has selected eight of the most common hair 'situations', including how to handle frizzy hair, hanging on to long hair for too long and going grey gracefully.

It's amazing what can be done with a light colour adjustment or a new style. Not all the changes needed to be dramatic. Richard explains what he has done, and why, in each instance.

So, go on, take a look in the mirror and ask yourself really honestly, 'Is this style doing for me what it should or is it time for a change?'

# HANGING ON TO LONG HAIR JESSICA

Having beautiful hair does not mean you should be tempted to keep the same long hairstyle that you have been wearing for years.

Keeping long hair won't necessarily mean you will look younger.

After the mid-thirties, a shorter haircut will make a woman look more sophisticated, smarter and more feminine. You can still have the feeling of long hair but with a more sophisticated look.

Richard Ward says: 'Jessica's hair had also been coloured at home and successive applications had given it a cold, dark look which very few skin tones or age groups can carry off. So we added some soft caramel slices and tinted the rest of the hair with a warm rich cocoa colour.

'We cut a good 4 inches off the length, hugely graduated the sides to give softness and cut a further 4 inches off the layers all over. This created a lot of movement and will give Jessica the feeling of still having longer hair.'

# OVERBLOWN BLONDE CAROLINE

Caroline's hair was a one-piece panel of solid blonde. The colour was too pale for her skin tone and didn't do justice to her eyes. The wrong tone of blonde can give a monotone effect, making hair, skin and eyes seem lifeless.

Richard Ward says: 'We broke up the colour with some coppery tones, taking it towards her natural light brown base. Then we added some light blonde caramel slices for contrast. We introduced layers, reducing the weight of the hair but keeping the length which elongates her face, making it appear more oval and less puffy. The overall effect is more sophisticated.'

The colours you wear will give you a hint about the right shade of blonde for you. If you wear cool tones you're more likely to suit an ash or beigy blonde. If you wear warm tones a rich golden or sandy blonde will suit you best.

# HELMUT HEAD DEBORAH

Often it is not the cut that is wrong, but style.

Richard Ward says: 'Deborah has been putting far too much volume in her hair and probably using rollers that are much too small. This was making her hair too bouffant and rigid and ageing her look.

'We've made her appear much younger purely by tweaking the haircut – chopping into the ends and the fringe to make it look less 'blocky' and styling her hair much straighter, which in turn makes her look younger.'

There is no excuse for having bouffant hair nowadays with so many straighteners on the market.

# GOING GREY GRACEFULLY MARGERY

Margery had never coloured her hair. Before turning grey, she was a light chestnut brown, so we wanted to bring those warm tones back into her hair, keeping the grey but adding several colours.

Richard Ward says: 'When thinking about the colours, we took into account that Margery's skin has a yellow undertone, her eyes are flecked with yellow, and her hair is a soft grey colour. So first we added a dark brown so her hair wouldn't look washed out.

Then came a golden light brown and two different beige blondes, one more golden than the other.

'If Margery had had a blue undertone to her skin, a cooler eye colouring and true salt and pepper hair, we would have added dark tones to reduce the grey. Either way, do not attempt to do this at home.'

Ask your hairdresser to do your parting and hairline around your face every 4–6 weeks and do your full head every 4–6 months.

# TEENAGE HAIR JUSTINE

Justine is a 30-year-old woman wearing her hair in the same style she wore when she was 16. She needs to try something more sophisticated and grown up which still leaves her with the feeling of long hair.

Richard Ward says: 'We've taken 3–4 inches off the length and layered the hair through with only long layers. We chopped into the ends of the hair to create movement which will encourage the hair to kick out.'

Justine had kept her hair long because she thought it didn't emphasise her round face, but you do not change your face shape with a hairstyle unless you take it above the jawline.

There is only one

It was invented b

It is called

the gui

cure for grey hair.
y a Frenchman.

llotine'

PG Wodehouse

Some women suit grey.
Others should find a
good hairdresser.

# FRIZZY HAIR RHONA

Rhona has frizzy, curly hair. She likes to wear
it long but has her layers cut far too short,
encouraging the hair to balloon and creating
volume and frizz. She can tame the wildness
by wearing the layers much longer which will
add weight to the hair and pull it down.

Richard Ward says: 'I want her to add
3 inches to her shorter layers at the top, so
she has some growing to do. Meanwhile we
have cut a couple of inches off the length.'

For the effect shown opposite, use Velcro
rollers which won't make the hair too straight –
they will just create a wave. If Rhona wants to
keep her hair curly, it can be finger-dried. As the
layers get longer, she can leave her hair to dry
naturally and the balloon effect will be vastly
reduced. Don't overdry your hair if making it
curly. You can let it dry naturally, using good hair
products to get the best effect. The key is to
reduce the frizz.

# ROOTS CAROLINE

Caroline is wearing her hair too blonde. The colour is very unforgiving so that when the roots come through they can be seen immediately.

Richard Ward says: 'We've changed the colour to something which is kinder to regrowth. For a busy woman who doesn't get the opportunity to touch up the regrowth every four weeks, this colour will give her 8–12 weeks without seeing obvious regrowth. We've also blow-dried Caroline's hair straight to give her a more modern look.'

If you have no grey, keep your natural colour on the top layer. Have highlights put in underneath so you won't notice the regrowth.

# SOFTENING YOUR LOOK NICOLA

Nicola hadn't found the right cut to suit her face or her hair. Her cut made her face look very rounded because her hair fell with a curtain effect over her forehead.

The Meg Ryan haircut has been popular for years and always will be. It's adaptable to most hair types because it is messy and unstructured, but it needs a perfect cut to make it work.

Richard Ward says: 'We cut the outside shape to jaw length and cut all over choppy layers to lift, soften and frame the face. It is a wash-and-wear haircut which can be finger-dried or blow-dried for a more dressy look.

'Her hair was also over-coloured. We added a mix of three colours that help define the texture and 'choppy' effect.'

' We too have made hair mistakes (even during the course of photographing this book). It's something you can never be lax about. Your hair is your crowning glory and it should be maintained. It's as important as underwear. '

# 10
# Make

They say that beauty is in the eye of the beholder. As far as we are concerned, the beholder needs to be blind or desperate ever to be attracted to our make-up-free faces. In the throes of the forties, we can no longer swish out the door with only a dab of moisturiser. Without make-up, we look like our faces have recently ploughed through a windscreen...all lined, red, blotchy and cratered.

Susannah used to pity her older sister for never leaving home without foundation. She believed that would never be her, in spite of subjecting her skin to extreme weather conditions and years of smoking. The writing was always on the wall for Trinny. Having suffered acne, she is well versed in the merits of concealer and art of facial disguise.

The irony is that while Susannah is the one blessed with good skin, Trinny is the one who always looks better on television and in photographs. Why? She is vain and very upfront about the fact. She LOVES make-up. She KNOWS how to apply the stuff and is on intimate terms with every new product. To say it is her obsession would be an understatement. So it is to her you must give the greatest nod of thanks for this chapter.

Susannah's contribution lies in recommending lazy ways with make-up for the girl who can't be bothered, has no time or hates the feeling of make-up on her skin. Thank Susannah for reducing the millions of products available down to the few we've highlighted in this chapter.

But the woman who has taught us the most, as well as telling us what to put in our make-up bags, has to be Charlotte Ribeyro. She has not only worked with us on our books and television series over the last few years but, more importantly, has also made us continuously aware of what we need to do.

The problem with make-up is that there is far too much choice. How on earth is a lay person supposed to wade through all those pigments, lipsticks, foundations, primers and preeners? What's the difference between cream and powder blush, oil-free and moisturising foundation? Should you opt for a skin perfector or a skin brightener, a skin tint or a skin refiner? Which products should you look for to cover spots, to make the most of your eyes or keep your make-up fresh all day? We make these recommendations and also show in graphic detail some of the most common make-up mistakes.

To so many of us the language of make-up is as foreign as Swahili. Beautiful sounding, but incomprehensible. That is why women so often give in to freebies and magazine giveaways. They don't care that the colour or the consistency doesn't suit them; the fact that they were free took away the fear of going into the cosmetics department and being sold something that wasn't what you wanted.

Make-up shopping is fraught with hazards. You might think you have hit the jackpot after reading a recommendation in a magazine. And, yes, that product probably is great and certainly looks so upon the fresh face of the 15-year-old model. Herein lies another peril. Once you've landed the brand of cosmetic, you need to know which products work for the age of your skin. For example, wrinkles should steer clear of powder, and spots should give a wide berth to anything that will leave any sort of residue. During menopause your body goes through many physical changes, but the worst are hot flushes. You need to be sure that your make-up won't streak at these times.

The age issue is one we have paid great attention to in this chapter, separating products into groups that are best for specific times in our lives. The thing you will benefit most from, however, is the fact that we have sorted through the make-up product maze for you. Unobstructed by advertising budgets or other commitments, we have picked only those products that in our down-to-earth opinion actually do the business.

# PREPARING YOUR SKIN

Some women's idea of preparing their skin for make-up is a bit of foundation or a dab of moisturiser; for others, it's a primer to keep foundation on and the skin oil free.

Taking the time to prepare your skin with certain products will make your foundation go on more smoothly, ensure it lasts longer and give a far better finish.

If your skin is not too sensitive, and you pile on the creams day in and day out, using a mask that takes away the build-up and dead skin cells will reveal a perfect pink glow to work with. Cleanse your face with Dr Sebagh's Deep Exfoliating Mask, followed with his Essential Glow and Crème Vital.

Beauty Flash Balm by Clarins can be used either as a mask thickly applied and then removed, or as a very thin layer that is left on, but it should not be rubbed too hard when the foundation is applied or bits come off on the skin. Rene Guinot's Masque Essential is great for a tired face, but remember to remove it with a hot flannel as it is too thick to get off successfully with water and hands.

If you suffer from sallow smoker's skin that can look rather grey, try a skin illuminator like La Prairie's Rose Illusion Line Filler or Estée Lauder's Spotlight. They both contain ingredients which give a reflective light to the skin to counter-balance the dull appearance created by too many late nights, smoking or just general fatigue.

A foundation primer, such as NARS Make-up Primer, generally allows your foundation to go on more smoothly and will make it last longer, especially if it is a hot day. Primer is a relatively new invention – you'll notice the difference at one in the morning.

**Top left to right** NARS Make-up Primer, Origins A Perfect World White Tea Skin Guardian, Clarins Beauty Flash Balm.
**Centre** Guerlain Issima Midnight Star Extraordinary Radiance Treatment, Dr Sebagh Deep Exfoliating Mask, SK-11 Facial Treatment Essence.
**Bottom** La Prairie Cellular Treatment Rose Illusion Line Filler, Estée Lauder Spotlight Skin Tone Perfector, Laura Mercier Secret Brightener.

# BROWS

A woman's face is framed by her brows. We have come across so many women whose biggest beauty blunder has been a lack of respect to the grooming of these face framers. Eyes can be opened up and the face entirely re-aligned by giving the brows a little tender loving care.

If you want to pluck your brows yourself, consider getting the set from Shavata. This renowned eyebrow expert has made up a fail-proof goody bag that includes the right shape brow you wish to achieve (an Elizabeth, a Kylie, etc) which you stick on your existing brow so you can pluck around the area. It's a complete fallacy that you shouldn't pluck above the brow, probably invented by some worried mother who thought her daughter might pluck over-zealously.

Some women prefer to put their brows in the hands of experts for threading, sugaring or waxing. If you do any of these, exfoliate for a week afterwards to make sure you get no in-grown hairs with the re-growth. Most importantly, let the beautician know how much you want removed.

If your problem is more a lack of hair than subduing the forest, make sure you use a brush and eyebrow colour in shadow form to fill in the cracks. There is nothing more unsightly (and ageing) than a badly applied pencil line in a slightly off-ginger hue replacing the bald patch.

**Tweezerman** slant tweezers.
**Left** Susannah's untidy brow.
**Right** Carefully plucked, Susannah's brows now open up her face, even with no eye make-up.

# SKIN

A flawless finish is what the bottle promises,
but if the product is badly applied the results
can be ageing, blotchy and draining to the skin's
natural colour. A well-applied base will ensure
that the rest of your make-up looks natural and
your skin glows.

When buying your foundation, don't get drawn
in by what it says on the bottle. Try it out on
your face, not your neck. (And why do people
insist on trying foundation on their wrist,
the palest part on the entire body?)
Take the make-up mirror
and go and check out the
colour in the daylight to
get a realistic view of
the coverage as well
as the colour.

Foundation should never be applied right under the eye to give thicker coverage; leave that work to the concealer. Always remember to smooth over and blend into the central part of your neck, which is generally paler than the rest of your face. A foundation's job is to even out the skin tone, and a concealer (which should be applied afterwards) is used to focus on more obvious flaws.

Deciding which consistency of a foundation is right for you will depend on the quality and age of your skin.

Women in their 20s may still be suffering from hormonal spots or acne, so they should lean towards an oil-free foundation. Gel-based foundations are better for those who need less coverage, but just a gentle evening out of tone.

Some foundations carry their own built-in skin illuminators so you don't have to buy a separate product.

If you have worn the same foundation for 10 years, check that it still does the trick. It might be time to move on. In the last five years a huge number of innovative products have come on the market, so it's really worth making the rounds in your local department store.

**From top to bottom** Chantecaille Real Skin (a good foundation for young and older skin); Laura Mercier Moisturising Foundation (gives a good coverage for older skin); Barbara Daly for Tesco make-up (available in oil-free and moisturising versions so something for all ages); Lancôme Transparence de Teint (good for the 20-30s age group); Prescriptives Traceless Skin Responsive Tint (suits skin of most ages).

# CONCEALER

For women with great skin and only a few imperfections, a concealer might be all that is required for a flawless finish. A celebrated make-up artist we have worked with believes that too many women cover themselves with foundation when all they really need is some strategically placed concealer.

We are not suggesting that you go out and buy yet more products, but if you suffer from dark circles as well as spots, you might consider buying two different concealers – one for under eyes and one for spots. Alternatively, use just one (for around the eyes) and blend it in with some of your foundation. Do this by dabbing it on with your fingertips – blending is the key to successful application.

A universally loved product has got to be Touche Eclat by Yves Saint Laurent, but be careful when applying it that you do not create light rings around your eyes. Far better to use it together with another, slightly darker, concealer (Touche Eclat is rather chalky in colour) and blend, blend, blend.

Cover-ups for scars and spots are thicker than those for around the eyes and need to be applied with a brush instead of the finger, which will take one dab to put on while the next will remove the coverage, ultimately leaving an unsightly build-up as you struggle to cover the offending area. Paula Dorf, Barbara Daly and Laura Mercier make great thin little brushes that do the trick.

When either of us have had a major zit outbreak, that Benefit's Boi-ing and Laura Mercier's Secret Camouflage have saved us.

**Top** Susannah's scarring (left) is completely covered with the application of Dermacolor Camouflage Make-up Mini-Palette. **Middle** Trinny's dark circles (left) are concealed with Yves St Laurent Touche Eclat, blended well with a little foundation. **Bottom** Spots can be concealed with a product such as Laura Mercier's Secret Camouflage.

# CHEEKS

Okay, the foundation is on, the spots are covered, and you no longer look like you need a week's rest to recover from your gallivanting lifestyle. Now a lot of women will go straight to the eyes and lips or attach the bronzing powder.

Wait a minute. How would you like to capture that flush of heathy outdoor youth, the 'I've just been fully satisfied in the bedroom' face? Well, blusher is your answer.

So many women get it so wrong that we feel the need to explain fully the benefits of avoiding the bronzer and going for the rosy cheeks look.

Much younger, chicer and less footballers' wives – we're sorry to categorise but they practically support the fake tan industry; blusher would be lost on their faces.

The key is to choose the blusher with the right colour and texture to suit your skin.

If you are younger with a great peaches and cream complexion, go for an apricot powder blush. Make apples of your cheeks (by grinning inanely) and apply with a brush. Using powder as opposed to cream blusher will allow the look to stay at least until the end of dinner.

For a more mature complexion, where the cracks are beginning to show, cream blusher looks more natural, especially if you also have a slightly downy face.

**Right** Good for dry skins and hairy faces are Stila Convertible in Rose and NARS Multiple Stick.
**Bottom right** Good for oily skins and hair-free faces are RMK Powder Blush and Bourjois Powder Blush.

**Susannah's** face without blusher (the left hand side) and with blusher (right), showing how the colour gives structure and rosiness to her face.

# LIPS

The number of unsuccessfully enhanced lips about only goes to show how many people are dissatisfied with the way they look. But you don't always have to resort to cosmetic surgery to remedy an unattractive pout.

As you get older, the appearance of lines above the mouth (particularly if you've ever been a smoker) can be one of the least attractive aspects of ageing. It is possible to diminish this problem.

Rubbing night cream vigorously into your lips will help (more in the Beauty chapter), but it is the fillers that go under your lipstick that make the most difference. Both The Body Shop's wax filler and Guerlain's lip lift fill in the lines sufficiently so that when covered with a lip gloss (avoid lipstick as it will run) the look is far smoother.

Thin lips can be a sign of meanness, but why let on when you can boost your natural pout with a bit of DuWop's Lip Venom. The cinnamon ingredients react against the skin and puff up the lip area. For best results, apply often.

To remedy a crooked mouth, a very careful application of the right coloured lip liner (we love MAC's lip pencil in Spice) should reduce the difference in size. Just be careful to blend liner well to avoid the drag queen lip liner look.

**From top to bottom** The product, and before and after: Guerlain Divinora Lip Lift will help to fill out lines. DuWop Lip Venom plumps up your pout. MAC Spice Lip Pencil helps even out the contours of your mouth.

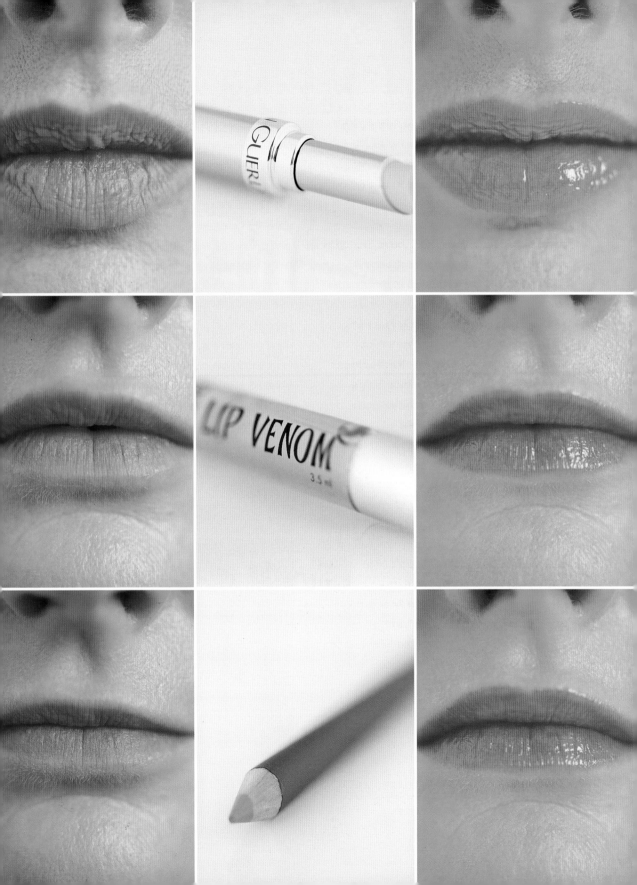

# EYES

The most commonly asked questions we get are: 'How do I apply eyeshadow?', 'How do I get rid of that greasy line that develops in my eye socket a couple of hours after I've applied my make-up? and 'What's the best mascara?'

These questions are from women who have been making up their faces for years. The trouble is that we get into a routine and it sticks. Our eyelids might droop, our hair colour might change and the wrinkles get deeper, but still we put on that heavy black kohl for the panda eyes look.

Well, it's time for a wake-up call. Sit down in front of the mirror with good natural light and look honestly at the windows to your soul. What do you see?

If your eyes are hooded, you need to use products that open up the area and enlarge the eye (which is probably getting lost among the folds). Brighten your entire under-eye area with YSL Touche Eclat, use smoky eye shadow to put a thickly smudged line on your top lid and curl your eyelashes; for extra impact at night-time, line the inner bottom ring of your eye.

If your eyes are deep set, use the flesh-coloured NARS Blonde Eyeshadow liberally over your lid, curl your eyelashes with a heated lash wand and apply a generous amount of mascara; for more drama, use Maybelline Cool Effects eyeshadow in your socket to define your eyelid further. The main thing to remember for deep set eyes is to keep sparkly eyeshadow to a

minimum because it will only make the rest of your eye recede even further.

If you suffer from bad lines around your eyes, apply Prescriptives Invisible Lines Smoother to the crow's-feet, then use Laura Mercier Eye Basic over the lid. This will give colour, but won't enhance the lines.

Try to steer clear of any powder products. If you want a bit of sparkle, try something such as Revlon Eyeglide Shimmer Shadow, but keep it close to the lash line. Curl your eyelashes and use mascara.

**For hooded eyes** Shu Uemura Eyelash Curler, YSL False Lash Effect Mascara, NARS Eyeliner Pencil, Bourjois Eyeshadow in Gris Magnetique and Eylure Individual Lashes.
**For deepset eyes** Estée Lauder MagnoScopic Mascara, ModelCo Lash Wand Heated Eyelash Curler, Maybelline Cool Effect Shadow/Liner Pencil and NARS Blonde Eyeshadow.
**For lined eyes** Tesco Eyelash Curler, Magic by Prescriptives Invisible Line Smoother, Laura Mercier Eye Basics, Revlon Eyeglide Shimmer Shadow and Maybelline Great Lash Mascara.

# NAILS

Your make-up is exquisitely applied, every hair on your head is glossy and shining…but look down at your nails. Are they chipped, bitten and dirty? No woman can really look her best if her nails are a mess. You don't have to cultivate long red talons – leave those to the beauty queens for scratching each other's eyes out. Just clean, neatly shaped nails with a gleam of flattering, even clear, nail varnish. And if you have nails that tend to break and flake, varnish actually does help to protect them.

The easiest way to keep your nails looking good is to go for regular manicures – and pedicures – but it's perfectly simple to DIY. Obviously you'll start by making sure your nails are sparkling clean and not looking like you've just dug potatoes with your bare hands. We all know not to use metal files, but did you know you can get glass nail files? These give a finer, gentler result and you can file in both directions. Otherwise use padded emery boards rather than the old-fashioned sandpaper types. Before applying polish, wipe your nails over with varnish remover to get rid of any grime or grease – helps the varnish go on better too. Always put on a base coat and top coat as well as your colour varnish. Reapply the top coat every couple of days to help it last.

Simpler still, polish your nails with a buffer which gives them a natural shine.

# Oh my...

'**A woman's first job is to choose the right shade of lipstick**'

**Carole Lombard**

**Some women don't even suit lipstick. Don't always think it's the one product that will 'cheer up' your face.**

# HOW TO KEEP YOUR MAKE-UP FRESH ALL DAY

Many a woman's answer to this is never to give it a chance to wear off in the first place. Long-lasting lipsticks that dry out, constant foundation plastering and powder overload – these don't make an attractive image. Far better to invest in some great products to freshen you and keep you on top of the situation.

A fab make-up primer will guarantee your make-up and foundation will last and stay looking smooth and airbrushed. In the afternoon when things start to look a little tired (perhaps), don't add more; simply work some Rosebud Salve into your fingertips and pat around the areas that need perking up and voilà, your base and face will regain its peachy glow.

Don't pile on the powder – it looks cakey and it's messy to carry around. Use blotting sheets to remove excess oil without product overload. Benefit's Dr Feelgood does the same trick and works well under or over your foundation.

Long-lasting lipstick is a crime. It does not look attractive to have a dried-on crust. Use normal products and if it's the ageing feathering that concerns you, prepare your lips with a waxy line filler like Body Shop Lip Line Fixer or Paula Dorf Perfect Illusion to make sure your lipstick stays where it ought to. Lipstick was not meant to last all day and the new natural, feather-light products are designed to be reapplied.

Eyeshadow debris? Lipline error? Simply whip out a ModelCo make-up remover bud and wipe away any mishap without the paraphernalia of cleanse, tone, moisturise. To refresh your face without splashing it with cold water, use a mineral mist which also fixes your make-up.

We love Crème de la Mer The Mist.

If you are having a long day at the office, followed by a night of excess, start the day with a good eye brightener applied under the eyes and in the corners of your nose. Benefit Ooh La Lift, Laura Mercier Secret Brightener and Guerlain Happology Eye Cream work wonders.

**Above** Stila mini brush set.
**Top left to right** Benefit Ooh La Lift, Laura Mercier Secret Finish, Body Shop Lip Line Fixer.
**Centre** Barbara's Private Collection Mineral Mist, Benefit Dr Feelgood Invisible Refiner, ModelCo Make-up Remover Cotton Buds.
**Below** Crème de la Mer The Mist, Smith's Rosebud Salve, Clinique Stay-Matte Oil Blotting Sheets.

This is the runway of cheek colour that whizzes down the cheek bone, a prerequisite for the inexperienced. Teenage girls, especially, often wear blusher that looks as if it has been applied by a painter and decorator. Many see the errors of their ways eventually, but many more don't, and are left looking dated and unsophisticated.

Those afflicted with the Roman road blusher look usually make the mistake of using the brush that comes with the blush. These are invariably too small and blunt-ended, making it impossible to get a soft coverage.

Using a colour that isn't suited to your natural skin tone also turns your blusher into an embarrassment. Blush is sold to enhance your colouring and make you look healthy and well. It is there to give definition to your cheek bones and NOT to define your whole face. Using a mismatched pigment is overpowering and theatrical. The end result must be less like Coco the Clown and more like Coco Chanel.

# CLASSIC MISTAKES MASCARA

We see a lot of this. So many women literally lacquer their lashes with layer upon layer of mascara. Why, we ask ourselves, do they do this? Of course the eyes are the mirror to the soul, but how the hell are you supposed to look in when they are curtained by thick black hairy spiders' legs?

The eyes are the most important feature of one's face. In surveys which ask men what physical attributes attract them to a woman, it's the eyes that come way up there...well, after tits, legs and arse. 'Oh, doesn't she have beautiful eyes,' is a line used when there isn't much else to compliment. 'It's in the eyes' is a phrase used to underline behavioural characteristics. Is it for these reasons that so much time goes into over-applying mascara?

Lots of women say they feel naked without mascara. This isn't surprising because thick lashes go a long way towards enhancing the eyes. What doesn't help is the addition of lumpy clumps that hang precariously from lashes, like skin tags you long to pull off.

We agree that at least two applications of mascara is a good idea, but they must be clog free. Wouldn't you rather have lashes that look naturally thick and glossy as opposed to resembling lumpy gravy?

Made-up lips should look natural. As soon as you start drawing an outline with a lip pencil it looks…well, drawn in. Regardless of the fact that so many of you do it, there is no earthly reason why a fake pout should be more appealing than the real thing. The whole point about make-up is that is should either look as natural as Elizabeth Arden will allow, or when piled on for a party, should be blended as if applied by a neo-classical painter.

The thing about lip liner is that no matter how flawlessly it is drawn on it will still look naff. If your lips are enclosed by a fence of dark pencil, they will look tiny, pinched and mean because you will have cut right into their fullness.

We think lip liners have a purpose, but one that is limited to dark lipsticks that need to be applied to the lips with great precision. Even in this instance, the pencil should be of exactly the same colour as the lipstick, otherwise no matter how clever you are, you will still muck it up.

There is no point in achieving a flawless skin with make-up if the foundation you are wearing doesn't match your skin tone. You might have a perfectly smooth shade of tawny on your face, but if this colour doesn't carry down over the jaw and onto your neck, the effect is disastrous. A tide mark of foundation along the jaw makes you look like you haven't had a bath in weeks and if you are prone to breakouts, the swampy, sticky residue is a perfect breeding ground for those spots.

In the same way that we forget to look at our rear view before leaving the house, whether through fear or genuine absent-mindedness, we forget that our neck is attached to our face.

Make-up can be like a mask, an illusion to give confidence, but it should be a disguise that only you are aware of. Show the world that your beauty was bought in a bottle, and you are suddenly less attractive.

The trick is getting one of the girls behind the make-up counter to help you match your foundation exactly to your skin. She should apply a smudge on your jaw line and if you can't see it, you have a good match. This will in turn make application so much easier and leave no room for dirty streaks.

Another instance where less is more. Eyebrows frame the face, and correcting brow imperfections can change a woman's appearance quite dramatically.

Too pale a brow leaves a face bland and devoid of definition, but too hard a line turns a girl into Groucho Marx.

Painting the brow in with a hard pencil also leaves the brow looking as if it has been stuck on like a false moustache.

Look at the Elizabeths Hurley and Taylor to see how attractive a beautifully arched brow can be.

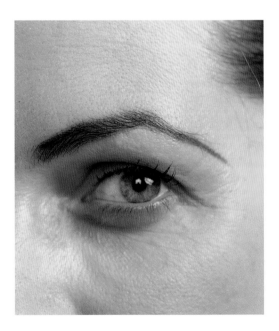

# CLASSIC MISTAKES BRONZER

It is lovely to feel healthy and well. It is almost more satisfying to look healthy and well. Blusher does this superbly, even on pale skins. Women who believe healthy living comes from a compact of bronzing powder or fake tan are absolutely right...if it's a Jaffa orange they are wanting to emulate.

A heavy hand armed with a bronzing brush gives the face the unreal aura of having been to the bronzing pot as opposed to the sun. An over-bronzed face becomes a façade that must be hiding a multitude of sins in a very unsubtle manner.

Leave your skin colour as nature intended. If you want a tan, get it in very small doses from the rays, rather than from crushed terracotta straight out of the potting shed.

# EMERGENCY

An emergency situation calls for drastic action. You've had a week of late nights already, but it's your best friend's wedding – you have to go! You look in the mirror and think to yourself, 'What beauty product can possibly save me?' As much as the product itself, your salvation lies in the skill with which you apply it.

The first thing you need to do is to give your face an invigorating massage. Start by pressing firmly with your fingertips from the centre of your forehead out to, and along, your hairline.

Next, for a really rosy cheeked moment, put your thumb in your mouth, pushing it as high up as possible inside your cheek cavity, then with your second and third fingers on the outside of your cheek, pull the the skin away from your mouth and across to your ear, really pressing the cheekbone quite firmly. Do it two or three times. Watch the rosy glow return to your face. It is advisable when practising this 'instant face-lift' to have short thumbnails.

After all this your face should have really woken up. For the final stimulation, take a good facial scrub (we love Korner's exfoliator or Jason Vita-C Max) and spend five minutes massaging it into your face. Then remove it with a really hot flannel. Rinse the flannel out and then sploosh your face again, this time with really cold water.

You are now ready to apply some of the products in Preparing Your Skin on pages 244-5.

# Help!!!

## £

Drink loads of water. Give your skin a really good massage to bring the circulation back and remove dryness. Put a couple of cucumber slices on your eyes.

## ££

Aveda Intensive Hydrating Mmasque

Darphin Instant Radiance Vitaserum

Elizabeth Arden Peel & Reveal

Estee Lauder Idealist Micro-D Deep Thermal Refinisher

The Organic Pharmacy Collagen Boost Antioxidant Gel Mask

Origins Out of Trouble 10 Minute Mask

Eve Lom Dynaspot

Jason Vita-C Max One Minute Facial

Origins Never A Dull Moment

## £££

Chantecaille Jasmine and Lily Healing Mask

Talika Eye Therapy Patch

Rodial Glam Balm

Crème de La Mer The Refining Facial

Jan Marini Clean Zyme Green Papaya Skin Cleanser

Jan Marini Skin Zyme Papaya Mask

Thalgo Youthful Look Patch Mask

Dr Sebagh Deep Exfoliating Mask, Essential Glow and Crème Vital

Dr Sebagh Serum Repair

Prescriptives Dermapolish System

Caudalie Vinotherapie Eye Lifting Serum

Eve Lom Rescue Mask

The Lift Petite facial mask

Korner the Exfoliator

**Clockwise from top** Jason Vita-C Max One Minute Facial, Eve Lom Rescue Mask, Jan Marini Clean Zyme Green Papaya Skin Cleanser, Jan Marini Skin Zyme Green Papaya Mask, Thalgo Youthful Look Patch Mask and Dr Sebagh Serum Repair.

'The older you are, the less make-up you should look like you are wearing, even though it might take you longer to apply. If you've worn the same make-up for the last five years, it's time to re-evaluate.'

S

# 11
# Travel

Having a good holiday lies in the preparation, and a happy return depends on how good you look in the holiday snaps. It matters not one iota that you are bound for the Barrier Reef if you have packed all the wrong things. Your home-coming, tanned and rested, will be unusually anti-climactic if you look like a pig in all the photographs. This may sound shallow and superficial to men and the naturally poised, but they haven't gone through the trauma of Bikini-Top-Left-Behinditis or always being caught at the wrong angle by a camera. To girls still stalked by puppy fat and us women plummeting into middle-age and beyond, the science of packing and posing is a subject that should be learnt.

We do appreciate that there are a few to whom packing means two thongs, a toothbrush and malaria tablets. These are drop-outs or eternal students on a quest for a spiritual wake-up call so don't pay any attention to them or use their Barbie-sized rucksacks as a yardstick by which to measure your trunk. Yes, it is nice to travel light, but that takes years of experience or an up-the-world attitude exclusive to the aforementioned drop-outs or the physically perfect. The bulk of us want to look our best, without standing out as the tourists we are. Having the correct clothing can really make or break a holiday.

There's nothing worse than going to a country and not bringing your favourite products because you didn't think there was room in your suitcase. Collecting samples of products you already use is better than taking the free samples of something you will never try. And take the time a few days before you go to decant your favourite beauty products into travel-sized containers.

One could say that Trinny was a gifted packer, in the sense that she can turn around two weeks' worth of clothes and pop them in however many suitcases it takes the night before departure. She has an eye for what's required and can glance through her wardrobes to select probably too much but everything she could possibly need, including an empty bag to carry all the stuff she'll buy once on vacation. She'll want for nothing and will live in a microcosm of the perfectly groomed. Susannah can attain the same results but hers is a more cultured method that requires a great deal of time and forethought. She likes to travel with the minimum. This means working out every outfit for every day prior to packing, and assuming that all countries are third world and unable to provide toothpaste, Tampax, shampoo, hairdryers, sun lotion, etc. Although she doesn't have the 'just-in-case' attitude, her suitcase will probably be the same size as Trinny's because in terms of sundries (anything other than clothes), she will have it all... including film and batteries for camera.

The camera can be the most dangerous beast that you encounter in foreign climes. It can kill all sense of decorum and shatter self-confidence just by poking its lens up your skirt, down your cleavage or deep into the folds of your stomach. Never, and we mean never, allow yourself to be too laid-back about having your picture taken. The lens is your enemy and has to be attacked with enormous amounts of posing done in a way that looks completely natural. When you are not perfect you cannot leave your photo appearance to chance...strike a pose and wear your favourite holiday kit to be sure of having glamorous not grungy memories of your precious free time.

Now, the journey itself. When you travel with small children and babies you have to think about practicality as well as comfort and style. When you're stuck on a plane for hours on end close to sticky fingers and flying drinks you don't want to have to worry about your velvet jacket or suede skirt. Think sensibly and wear colours that won't show up dirt and grime, and fabrics that can be chucked in a washing machine as soon as you arrive – looking like the chocolate mousse served for your airline meal.

# MINIMISING YOUR TOILETRIES

The clothes are packed, you close the suitcase, test the weight, and oh, by Jove, it's really not that heavy. Wow, how fab. You might even be able to sneak it on as hand luggage. And then you put in your sponge bag, followed by sun lotion, shampoo and beachbag. Next comes the make-up, which you implant carefully down the side where there is a small space between your knickers and flip-flops. You squeeze the case closed and perform another lift test. Your arm is pulled from its socket. You spend the two-week vacation strapped up with a shoulder dislocation.

It's always the toiletries that bugger up your carefully laid packing plans. They weigh more than anything else, invariably leak and are usually left behind half-full at the end of your holiday because you can't be arsed to carry them back home.

Have you ever heard of miniature sizes or the method of decanting beauty stuff into lightweight plastic containers?

Let us introduce you to the joys of less-is-more-room for sexy tops and sundresses. The collation of miniature products doesn't happen overnight. It can be hard to find what you need in small form. You have to keep your eyes peeled at every chemist, supermarket and beauty counter for mini-versions of your favourite cosmetics. If they are not on display, ask for them and never turn down a free sample, however annoying the woman handing them out might be.

Fortunately, cosmetic companies have begun to meet the demand for travel sizes. You can get pretty much everything from shampoo to toothpaste and even body scrubs in titchy bottles or sachets. The beauty of baby-sized products is that they are lighter, take up less room and avoid wastage.

**Above** These are the products we pack in our holiday sponge bags. Brands we like are shown here, but you will have your own favourite versions.

**Top row** body lotion, bath oil, lip gloss, foundation.

**Middle row** shampoo, conditioner, skin tonic, body mist, tinted moisturiser, day cream, cleanser.

**Bottom row** toothpaste, deodorant, hair styling lotion, after sun cream, sun screen.

**Right** Most of the above come in mini versions or sample sizes. Those that don't, we decant into little bottles and jars from Muji.

# HOW TO PACK A SUITCASE

Amazingly, it is Susannah who has perfected the art of packing a suitcase. Not the actual physical packing of the clothes (that she learnt from Trinny), but the ability to take only what she needs and get it into a hold-all small enough to slide into the overhead lockers on a plane. This miraculous feat was born from a desire always to avoid putting her luggage in the hold. Waiting at the carousel while baggage handlers idle back from lunch or are on strike became a nightmare, when all Suz wanted to do was get back to her family as quickly as possible.

Small-time packing is much easier, and to be honest only truly possible, in the summer. The light fabrics fold into nothing. Coats and jackets are unnecessary and one's footwear is much less clumpy.

When travelling to a colder climate, the trick is to wear all the bulky stuff, like warm coat and boots, on the flight. The boots should be smart enough for business and flat enough to wear day in, day out. These need to be accompanied by one pair of heels for the evenings.

When it comes to the actual filling of your suitcase you must rid yourself of the stereotypical method of putting the heavy stuff at the bottom so that it doesn't squash your clothes. The best way is the reverse. If you put all the hardware on top, it acts as a press and keeps the clothes beneath unable to wriggle around and get creased. It also means there are more nooks and crannies in which to stuff last-minute bits and pieces.

Lots of small items and clothes folded flat or into tiny bundles are more packing friendly than one big puffa or jumbo cord trousers.

**Top** Put heavy items on top to keep everything else in place.
**Centre** Place folded items, such as tops and jackets, in the middle layer.
**Bottom** Start by placing the items that you want to remain flat, such as trousers and skirts.

# WHAT TO CARRY LONGHAUL

There is no getting away from the fact that longhaul flights are completely awful. Twelve hours of compressed air filled with other people's germs and a seat that turns buttocks into hard, overcooked minced beef makes you wonder whether two weeks on a beach is worth the agony of the flight. This is a natural attitude but one that you have to get over. If you think of your aeroplane seat as a bedroom and equip it accordingly, the journey will be much improved.

**A cabin-sized bag** can carry everything you need on the flight as well as reading matter. These are our essentials.
**Top row opposite** pashmina (folds into nothing and is warmer and less smelly than an airline blanket), eye mask, toothbrush and toothpaste, cashmere socks (warm and won't make your feet sweat).

Think of the essentials you need for a good night's sleep. If it's a pill, take one. If it's a soft pillow, take that too. If your feet tend to get chilled, bring warm socks on board, and if you are germ-phobic, spray your space with tea-tree oil.

Prepare yourself as you would at bedtime. This ritual will help you relax and make you feel at home. Take off your make-up, brush your teeth. Have a hot drink, then take a pee. Be comfortable in your clothes or even change into pyjama-type bottoms. You will look totally mad doing all these things, and you won't be picked up by a handsome stranger while you have wax in your ears, an eye mask and a dribbling chin from the deep sleep your pre-flight planning has promoted. But you will arrive refreshed.

**Centre row below** compact with a little mirror, Jurlique Rosewater Skin Freshener (wonderfully refreshing), Stress Mints (homeopathic stress remedies in mint form), Guerlain Midnight Secret (the best, but most expensive, flight hydration cream), flannel, ear plugs.

**Bottom row** neck pillow, mouthwash, homeopathic jet lag remedy, eye drops, Domomyl (herbal sleep aid), Organic Pharmacy herbal in-flight spray, Rescue Remedy (for those scary bumpy moments, spray vitamins (easy to absorb and gentler on the stomach than tablets), Evian water.

'Modern travelling is it is merely being and very little becoming a

not travelling at all;
sent to a place,
different from
parcel.**"**

John Ruskin

If you are a parcel,
at least be well wrapped. **S**

# HOW TO LOOK GOOD IN HOLIDAY PHOTOGRAPHS

Most people feel stupid posing for a photo. It's hardly surprising when you see the results – chins descending into cleavage, legs looking six inches long, stomach settling into rolls. It takes guts to go for the pose that flatters your body to its best advantage because posing gives away the fact that you feel less than perfect. But, while it is embarrassing the first few times, it becomes second nature. Soon you will always look your best, and what bliss to have the advantage over those who are younger, thinner and prettier than you simply by being stunningly photogenic and a gift to all amateur snappers.

## BIG TITS

Big boobs can very quickly turn to fat unless they are manipulated into shape with good posture. You must never lean forwards to bunch them together as this looks cheap and too porn star (if you are young) or barmaid (if you are old, like Susannah here). What you must do is thrust them out by keeping your shoulders back.

We don't mean an arched page three thrust but one that is more relaxed, a stance that is achieved by keeping the arms limp. If the tits are held forwards they don't merge into any fat folds elsewhere.

# NO TITS

The last thing you want to look like in your holiday snaps is a man in drag. You don't want your bikini top to look pointless, with the two triangles empty of anything to grasp hold of. If you do get caught by a roving camera lens while lying on your back, your tits (what there is of them) will disappear under your arms and look like pectorals instead of breasts. You'll look like a body builder as opposed to a glamorous beach babe. Sit up, for goodness sake. Keep your back straight and arms away from your sides so that your little mounds don't become part of your arms. Easy to do and you'll be amazed at the results.

# SHORT LEGS

If you don't like your legs you may have a tendency to try to tuck them away underneath the chair or whatever you may be sitting on – anything to keep them away from a prying camera. Unfortunately your embarrassment is doing your legs no favours. They'll look a foot shorter if the only part you can see is your calves. You can so easily extend the leg by showing more flesh. Part them and camouflage with a casual hand or dangling hat. It's really that newborn foal or Bambi stance that we're after. One where your pins have the look of being too thin to carry your torso.

# BIG ARMS

We do believe that these should be covered whenever possible, but there are occasions when this is just not an option. On the beach is that time. Suddenly to reach for a sarong to cover them would be too much and not possible anyway with something in your hand. And it's the something in your hand that is the essential ingredient for a thinner limb. If you are carrying sunglasses, hat or a drink, it looks more natural to have the free mitt casually placed upon your hip. Keeping some distance between the arm and your body leaves room for fat to dangle down out of the way.

# NO WAIST

This is a no brainer. Simply use your hands as a corset to winch in that non-existent curve. Your action will automatically make you stand better and create a dent in the sides of your torso.

# SADDLEBAGS

Disguising this problem is a little more contrived because it means asking the photographer to move positions and take the picture from behind. You, in turn, have to distort your neck, providing a clear view of your face for the camera. Taking a picture from this angle elongates the legs. Just don't forget to lift your thighs away from the sun lounger so that, as with fat arms, the superfluous flesh hangs down and stays well out of sight.

# FLABBY TUMMY

There is no real trick to ridding yourself temporarily of a big tum. You can't suck it away, and turning your back to the camera (the only cast-iron method of being rid of a tummy) is, well, pointless. You can, of course, sling something over it, but that becomes too obvious after the tenth picture of you with a towel draped over your middle. The best suggestion we can offer (and we admit it's not fail-safe) is to lie flat, suck in and hold your breath with a big smile that defies the agony you're going through to pull that pose.

# NO NECK

If your neck is less than swanlike, an unwary snap can leave you looking like your head comes straight from your shoulders.

The solution below is a balance between getting the neck to appear longer without the lens heading straight up your nose, which can make the loveliest of us look uncannily equine.

When the camera threatens, take a moment to strike a reasonable pose – you'll thank us for this later. Lie with your head tilted back slightly and your chin up and you will be surprised how elegant your neck will look. Make sure you are still below the level of photographer and camera to avoid horsey nostrils.

'Anything can happen on a foreign journey, so the more planning you do to look great the more prepared you will be to face any situation.'

**12**

# Pregn

There is no getting away from the fact that being pregnant takes a while to get used to. Feet and pubes become a figment of some distant past when you were able to see them. Sleeping silently on one's back is replaced by lying in a fortress of pillows and snoring loudly enough to awake the neighbours and yourself.

Although we've been lucky in all our collective pregnancies in terms of health, our happiness was thwarted slightly by feelings of hurtling through something resembling a mid-life crisis.

We can make most tummies disappear, but there are limits...pregnant stomachs being one. The thing is, with protruding bellies, there is no getting away from the fact that we were not up for grabs. It's not like you can pretend to be young, free and possibly single. This means any thoughts of flirting with boys young enough to be 'nephews' need to be shelved. Even as the proverbial 'older woman', we are not an option when we look and feel very like wet sandbags.

Tiresome though this temporary confinement on our sexuality was, we found other ways to amuse ourselves. The first and most enjoyable was simply to give in to food. The second was finding ways to look decent enough for our husbands, who are funnier and better looking than any tiresome youths, to continue to fancy us. Ironically, the latter was easier for Susannah because her obsession with clothes is not a life or death condition. Imagine how hard it was for Trinny, to whom fat is an alien nation and fashion her heart's blood, watching her skinny frame bursting the seams of immaculate outfits.

Pregnancy highlights and expands what you hate about your body. Having tits and tum as problem areas anyway, made pregnant life smoother for Susannah because these are the areas that get bigger naturally when having a baby (in case any woman hasn't noticed!). Adapting her look was simply a question of extending her existing garments. Trinny, on the other hand, had to cope with elephantine legs, broadening hips *and* a swelling tummy and tits, a fact that really did her head in for a while.

In spite of clothes getting tighter, our resolve never to touch maternity wear remained unbroken. We once walked into one of those shops where the mannequins have balloon-like growths and vowed never to return.

Why would any woman with child want to make herself look not just like a tent, but the whole camp? The real turn-off was those trousers with the specifically engineered panels. Once we were both four months into gestation, our irregular shapes forced us towards pregnancy jeans. All we can say is that Earl Jeans had the last laugh on Susannah as she lived in the two pairs bought with excited relief, while Trinny, ever the true style guru, got her trousers specially fitted by a handy dressmaker.

Anyone who's had a baby will know that one remains pregnant for a few weeks after giving birth, so don't assume you can pack away the clothes you wore while you were pregnant; they will stand you in good stead afterwards. This is depressing, but there is no point in buying anything new for at least three months post birth. If you need retail therapy, which you invariably will, especially after looking at yourself naked in front of a full-length mirror, splash out on clothes for your baby or buy really expensive accessories for yourself.

Once you have had the baby, and if you are breastfeeding, your teats will leak, so avoid anything too pale which will show up moisture like sweat marks under your arms. And don't wear anything that's too tight around the waist.

Pregnancy is a tough one to combat in all respects, but if you look good then, everything in life becomes so much more pleasurable. It was a challenge for us, but one we thoroughly enjoyed.

# WINTER CASUAL WEAR

It is so easy to slide into the murky world
of husband's shirts and comfy leggings when
pregnant. Nobody, however marvellous,
beautiful, perfect and thin they are, looks
dignified submerged in a baggy button down and
saggy-arsed, footless tights. This combination is
offensively awful and an injustice to the beauty
of the pregnant form. If your legs remain skinny,
and more importantly your butt doesn't get too
huge, show them off in tightish trousers and
your bump in a skinny top. At least
then you will look pregnant as
opposed to deformed.

Have you ever seen Trinny look as ghastly as she does in this jump suit? The fact that she can stand there with a straight face is in itself quite remarkable. Her arse, already not her best feature, is blown out of all proportion when encased in padded nylon. She needs to show her bump in relaxed, fitted, lightweight wool, with cosy wide-leg pants that envelop her ever-increasing, child-bearing hips.

# you've got to be joking!

# WINTER WORK WEAR

Susannah loves the idea of a dress over trousers. What a shame then that she looks so vile in this useful and stylish clothing concept. Why? Well, the dress tents her stomach, hiding the skinniest part of her big form – her hips and bum. This is the very reason the tight figure-hugging dress works so well. It proudly displays that her stomach is so huge there could be a whole litter nestling within its vastness.

Poor Trinny's legs suffered terribly during pregnancy. Words like swollen, elephantine, city-servicing water-tank retention can be accurately used to describe her lower half in this skirt. You would not think they were the same legs in this comely long jacket that hides it all. The heels add length to her stumps, which in these long trousers look lithe and elegant...no mean achievement.

# WINTER EVENING WEAR

Susannah looks like she could hide a three-
seater sofa up her skirt. Do look at how
enormous this billowing chiffon makes her
appear. This may be one fancy skirt she can
get into, but so could all the other guests...
at the same time. A pregnant stomach
enveloped in a small print has its size diffused,
while the legs can continue to carry off jeans,
albeit pregnancy ones.

Even when pregnant, Trinny just cannot afford to wear a dress so tight that it shows where her bum ends and short stumpy legs begin – in fact, pregnancy makes it worse. But she can wear a dress over trousers. As when not carrying, she still needs to try to shorten her back and lengthen her legs, which this outfit does by neatly disguising her bottom.

# WINTER PARTY WEAR

Pregnancy is the only time Susannah's fat arms are allowed on show and that's because they look relatively small beside her enormous breasts. She cannot, however, be seen dead in a strappy little number, because the smallness of the dress makes her huge frame look even larger. Much better for Suz to keep things long, tight and streamlined.

You have got to give it to her – the girl is brave to be photographed in these salami-leg-turning tights and this sausage-like, skin-tight dress. Trinny would look great in the window of a butcher's shop, but not at a film premiere. For her, the dress-over-trouser theme continues to work beautifully for camouflaging her botty and legs.

**'I didn't have to buy any new outfits when I was pregnant; I just went to my husband's wardrobe'**

Anonymous

I wonder how long
that marriage lasted.

S

# SUMMER CASUAL WEAR

Many young mums-to-be adopt the 'let it all hang out' approach. Not us. We are too old and too square for that. It is hard to be casual and cool while keeping comfortable and looking relaxed. That's why Susannah lives in sarongs during summer pregnancies (she sounds like a brood mare). They can be tied to fit precisely and they look great with a fun T shirt and flat gold or silver flip-flops or Birkenstocks.

As soon as Trinny does floaty skirt or dress without the trousers she looks like she might take off. For her thickening ankles, trousers were the only option, and as her arms remained unaffected by baby, she was able to show them off in simple vests. A nice clean outfit like this is a great solution for those wanting comfort and practicality.

# SUMMER WORK WEAR

It's not easy to look smart at work while remaining cool. Susannah found the ideal solution in tight-fitting dresses with cardigans. Tempted towards crisp cotton skirts, she was soon put off by the fact she resembled a pot-bellied pig dressed in human clothes. Fabrics with a bit of stretch have the bonus of remaining crease free.

When it's hot and you are with child, the
appeal of pretty summer dresses is irresistible.
You think of the lovely draughtiness they provide
and the earth-motherliness they represent. But
they can sadly damage your reputation at work
because, being voluminous, they billow like sails
over the bump. If you carry your weight down
below and want to be pretty yet professional,
wrap your belly in flowers and, as ever, stick the
pack atop a pair of casually fitting trousers.

# not from here
# honey!

# SUMMER EVENING WEAR

Oh, it's so lovely to go ethnic in the summer,
but you have to choose your country of influence
cleverly when shaped like Susannah. As she
so clearly demonstrates, big-tented tops make
her look frumpy and ready for the forceps.
A slim-line kaftan, belted under the bump,
looks relaxed, fun and much more flattering.

As soon as that butt goes on display it all starts to go horribly wrong. The combination of tight top and trousers shows that Trinny's bottom is as big as the baby-carrying tummy. Yet again, the dress-over-trousers look, and one that shows off her temporarily large breasts, is boosting both emotionally and physically.

# SUMMER PARTY WEAR

Never be lured into thinking that flowers and froth work if your boobs are as big as your belly. Even at normal, lactating-free moments, big prints do nothing for large breasts other than make your assets look bloated. Think back to the everyday rules of boob dressing and keep the colours monochrome and the shapes slim and simple.

Just because your shape has changed, don't
go thinking you can suddenly wear clothes that
didn't suit you before. A bias-cut skirt or dress
has never been Trinny's friend, and it never will
be. When you are pregnant, summer lightness
only works when the print is small or subtle.
Because you are larger, large blossoms make
every mother-to-be look bigger than she needs to.

# GOOD BRA

There is only one make of bra that is pretty, uplifting and easy to whip a tit out from and that is the one designed by Elle MacPherson. It comes in a range of colours and is as comfortable as a second skin. Really fabulous.

# GOOD SUPPORT

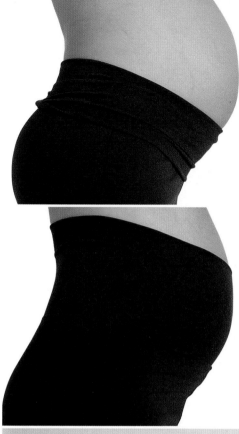

When your baby becomes sodding heavy, a bit of support for your back and pelvis is a help if you are having to do a lot of standing around.

# GOOD TROUSERS

We both found these sweatpants (from Christy Turlington's Nuala range by Puma) a lifesaver. The supportive stretch front panel and roll-down waistband can be worn low or up over the bump.

# PRODUCTS

If your mum is still around, ask her how her body behaved during pregnancy. If it suffered from stretch marks, water retention, sickness, acne outburst or any other such changes, the chances are you will too.

Simulcium G3 cream (right) is the answer for anyone in fear of stretch marks. You must be consistent and rub it in nightly.

Micheline Arcier's aromatherapy bath oils, New Breath, are great for softening the skin.

There is no sadder time than the end of breast-feeding for a girl like Trinny. But don't despair, try Sisley's bust cream, called Phytobuste, and the elasticity – if not the generous cup size of your pregnant days – will return.

'You don't have to lose your sense of style just because you are pregnant. It's worth making that extra effort for the compliments you will receive.'

S

# S&T'S TOP 10 BEAUTY PRODUCTS

## SUSANNAH'S TOP 10 PRODUCTS

**01** Cotton face flannel and water.
The simplest beauty aid of all. Easy and always available wherever I go in the world.

**02** Dr Hauschka Rose Day Cream. First and foremost, I love the smell of this cream, but it's also an intensive moisturiser that doesn't make my skin too sticky

**03** Jo Malone green tea and honey eye cream. My eyes are very sensitive to most eye creams. This is the only one that doesn't make them water.

**04** Eye Dew. After a late night my eyes get terribly red and bloodshot which is a complete giveaway. Eye Dew covers my alcoholic tracks.

**05** Esthederm Sea & Tropics suntan lotion, available at Space NK. I suffered from heat rash all my life until I found this product. Now, for the first time, I actually go brown.

**06** Weleda Rose Body Lotion. The consistency is thin, which makes it very quick and easy to apply but the softening effect is quite extraordinary.

**07** Neutrogena Sesame Body Oil. If I'm in a rush, applying this oil to my wet skin is the easiest way to moisturise. It's especially good for summer holidays.

**08** Eve Lom The Cleanser. I know that this is more than just a cleanser but I love to use it for cleaning my face when it's been laden with make-up.

**09** N.V. Perricone ALA Face Firming Activator. In my view, this is the only product that goes a tiny way towards arresting the ageing process. I am a real sceptic but I do think this works.

**10** Crème de La Mer The Lotion. As well as smelling delicious, this is a wonderfully light moisturiser that I find especially good for the summer months.

## TRINNY'S TOP 10 PRODUCTS

**01** Eve Lom The Cleanser. I've used this for the last 15 years. It helped my recovery from acne, and the cleansing massage technique she teaches really keeps my face toned and youthful.

**02** Jason Vita-C One Minute Facial. I use this wonderful exfoliant daily to help ward off the wrinkles that threaten us all sooner or later.

**03** Jan Marini C-Esta serum. I use this Vitamin C-infused product after cleansing. It's a natural barrier for the sun and a very good base for absorbing the products I put on top.

**04** Jan Marini Bioclear Cream. I put this on nightly and I feel it has helped keep my spots at bay as well as sloshing off all my dead skin cells.

**05** Guerlain's Midnight Secret. Although prohibitive in price, I use this sparingly whenever I travel to avoid the chronic dehydration effects longhaul flying has on my skin.

**06** Dr Sebagh Deep Exfoliating Mask. If you don't have time, or the cash, to go to Dr Sebagh's surgery for a treatment, this mask does the trick.

**07** Jan Marini Daily Face Protectant SPF 30. There are few products that protect your skin from the sun's harmful rays without covering your face in a white film. This is one of them.

**08** La Mer The Face Serum. I put this on in the morning after cleansing and as well as making my skin feel great, it tightens everything just enough.

**09** Guerlain Issima Hand Care. This hand cream smells divine. I put it on at night and when I wake up in the morning my hands still feel incredibly moisturised.

**10** Estée Lauder Light Source Age-Resisting Eye Cream. This entire range reflects light from the face. Especially good when I haven't slept well and have even darker circles under my eyes.

# S&T'S TOP 10 MAKE-UP PRODUCTS

## SUSANNAH'S TOP 10 PRODUCTS

**01** Laura Mercier Moisturising Foundation. The only foundation I've been able to find that goes on perfectly and gives me naturally smooth-looking skin.

**02** Lâncome Juicy Tubes. I never wear lipstick but I feel that my lips always look fresh and clean with a slick of this gloss. I carry one of these everywhere.

**03** Stila Eyeshadow in Starlight. The colours are pale enough for me not to make a mess with this, yet it's shimmery enough to really make my eyes stand out.

**04** Stila Convertible Colour in Rose. I love this product. It is a fantastic blush for giving me that 'I've just been for a healthy walk in the fresh air' rosiness.

**05** Spa.NK Waterproof Mascara. For me, it's the only mascara I've ever used that doesn't clog and make nasty lumps on my eyelashes.

**06** Smith's Rosebud Salve. Inexpensive and comes in a lovely, old-fashioned tin. I put this on my cheekbones over my foundation and blush for a dewy youthful glow.

**07** Stila Eye Glaze. A great shadow for when I can't be bothered to put anything else on but I want a finished look to my face.

**08** Chanel Irreelle Blush in Secret. A light, pressed powder blusher and my favourite for the evening. Gives me a subtle glamorous glow.

**09** Benefit Boi-ing Industrial Strength Concealer. I've never found a better match to my skin tone than this under-eye concealer. Covers dark circles with ease.

**10** Screenface individual false lashes in black. I can't put these on by myself so I only wear them for special occasions when Charlotte is at hand. Nothing gives my face more glamour.

## TRINNY'S TOP 10 PRODUCTS

**01** Chantecaille Future Skin foundation. I tried hundreds of foundations before finding this. The colour is perfect, and I use it as a fine day-time base and for heavier evening coverage too.

**02** Chantecaille Total Concealer. This concealer has an extremely good texture while still giving good coverage. I don't feel that it's heavy.

**03** YSL Touche Eclat. I have stopped using this on its own because I find it too chalky, but mixed with another concealer it gives great reflective coverage for my dark shadows.

**04** Lâncome Juicy Tubes. I keep these in every area of my life: my car, my bathroom, my office, all of my handbags...for fear of ever being without.

**05** Laura Mercier eyeshadow in Lavender Mist. This looks like a strong purple but it gives a very subtle dusting of colour. I use it at night over a smudged brown pencil to soften the look.

**06** Paula Dorf Perfect Illusion lipline filler. Although I have large lips, talking a lot, and smoking in my youth, have taken their toll so I need something to fill those ridges. This does the job.

**07** Calvin Klein brown eyeliner pencil. I haven't found any other pencil that is as successfully smudgy as this one. It has a sponge at one end to soften the line.

**08** YSL False Lash Effect mascara. I find that this one is extremely uncloggy, although I still always wipe my mascara wand with a tissue before applying it to my lashes.

**09** Paula Dorf Eyebrow Gel in clear. As I get older, I find that my eyebrows are becoming more and more unruly. This gel is a great tidier-upper.

**10** Laura Mercier tweezers. These tweezers, made in conjunction with Tweezerman, have an extremely good grip and make plucking eyebrows that much easier.

# THE DIRECTORIES

## 02 UNDERWEAR

### £

H&M
Gap Body
Knickerbox
La Senza
Marks & Spencer
Peacocks
Sloggi
Topshop
Valisere

### ££

Aubade
Bodas
Bravissimo
Calvin Klein
Coco Ribbon
Elle Macpherson Intimates
Fantasie
Figleaves.com
Freya
Gossard
Huit
Lejaby
Love Kylie
Ultimo
Warners
Wolford
Wonderbra

### £££

Agent Provocateur
Cacharel
Damaris
Exotica of Brazil
FrostFrench
Hanro
Janet Reger
La Perla
Magic Knickers
Myla
Rigby & Peller
**Specialist Underwear**
Bravissimo – large sizes
Goddess – large back and cup sizes
La Senza – breast enhancers
Myla – breast enhancers
Ultimo – silicone bras

---

## 03 COLOUR

### £

Benetton
Esprit
French Connection
Gap
H&M
John Lewis
Kookaï
Matalan
Miss Selfridge
Monsoon
Morgan
New Look
Oasis
Pilot
Topshop
Warehouse
Zara

### ££

Cacharel
Georges Rech
Ghost
Jigsaw
Juicy Couture
John Smedley
Karen Millen
Marc by Marc Jacobs
Megan Park at The Cross
Miss Sixty
Pringle
Sara Berman
Velvet
Whistles

### £££

Alberta Ferretti
Alexander McQueen
Ann-Louise Roswald
Balenciaga
Betsey Johnson
Blumarine
Celine
Chloé
Diane von Furstenberg
Dolce & Gabbana
Emilio Pucci
Etro
Kenzo
Marc Jacobs
Marni
Matthew Williamson
Missoni
Paul Smith
Roberto Cavalli
Sybil Stanislaus
Temperley
TSE
Tulah at A la Mode
Versace

## Boutiques and shops with a great eye for colour

**London**
? Air – NW3, SE21, SW13, SW19 & W11
The Abbey – SW4
A la Mode – SW3
Anna – NW1
Brown's – SW3 & W1
Club – SW1
Cochinechine – NW3
The Cross – W11
Diverse – N1
Feathers – W11 & SW1
Fenwick – W1
Frock Brokers – E14
Genevieve – NW11
Hannah Lee – NW8
Harvey Nichols – SW1
The Jacksons – W11
Joseph – W1, WC2, W11, SW3 & NW8
Koh Samui – WC2
Liberty – W1
Linea – NW3
Matches – W11
Mimi – SW3
Nawar – N6
Powder – N8
Shop – W1
Sixty 6 – W1
Sublime – E9
Wilson – SW4
**Bath**
Jaq
Square
**Birmingham**
Flannels

Harvey Nichols
Katherine Draisey – Solihull
**Brighton**
Mottoo
Simultane
**Buckinghamshire**
Chattertons – Old Amersham
**Cambridge**
Giulio
Hero
**Cheshire**
Garbo – Wilmslow
**County Durham**
Joseph M – Darlington
**Dublin**
Brown Thomas
Smock
**Edinburgh**
Corniche
Cruise
Harvey Nichols
**Essex**
Blue Lawn – Chelmsford
Choice – Romford
Peep Show – Buckhurst Hill
**Exeter**
Willy's
**Glamorgan**
Square Spots – Cowbridge
**Glasgow**
Cruise
**Gloucestershie**
The Linen Press – Moreton-in-Marsh

**Guildford**
The Courtyard
**Hampshire**
Moda Rosa – Alresford
**Kent**
The Changing Room – Tunbridge Wells
Joseph – Bluewater
Little London – Tunbridge Wells
**Lancashire**
Garbo – Wigan
Velvet
**Leeds**
Harvey Nichols
Strand
**Leicestershire**
Doyle's – Market Harborough
**Liverpool**
Cricket
Wade Smith
**Manchester**
Flannels
Harvey Nichols
**Merseyside**
Garbo – Southport
**Newcastle**
Cruise
**Norwich**
Catherine Barclay
Two Stars
**Norfolk**
Anna – King's Lynn
**Northampton**
Thackery's

| **Nottingham** | **Surrey** | **Winchester** |
| --- | --- | --- |
| Flannels | Bernard's – Esher | Hambledon |
| Milli | Footlights – Cobham | **York** |
| **Oxford** | Lucy's – Weybridge | Sarah Coggles |
| Vanilla | **Sussex** | East Yorkshire |
| **Somerset** | East Street – Petworth | Riley's – Beverley |
| Lu Lu Anderson – Babbington | **Warwickshire** | **North Yorkshire** |
| **Suffolk** | Mosaique – Stratford-upon-Avon | Lynx – Harrogate |
| Anna – Bury St Edmunds | **West Midlands** | The Clothes Room – Harrogate |
| Tulip – Southwold | Madeleine Ann – Solihull | Morgan Clare – Harrogate |

## 04 CULLING

| **No hassle** | British Heart Foundation | **Some hassle but worth it** |
| --- | --- | --- |
| Jumble sales | British Red Cross | Car boot sale |
| Recycling bin | Cancer Research UK | Market stall |
| Charity shops – check your local Yellow Pages | Marie Curie Cancer Care | Swap party – see No Cost Wardrobe |
| Age Concern | Oxfam | **Dress agencies & vintage clothing stores** |
| All Aboard | SCOPE | Check your local Yellow Pages |
| Barnardo's | TRAID | |

## 06 ACCESSORIES

| £ | ££ | £££ |
| --- | --- | --- |
| **Bags** | | |
| Accessorize | Aftershock | Anya Hindmarch |
| John Lewis | Coccinelle | Balenciaga |
| Marks & Spencer | French Connection | Billy Bag |
| Topshop | Furla | Burberry's |
| Woolworths | J Maskrey | Chanel |
| Vintage bags from Oxfam and other charity shops | Lúki | Chloé |
| Zara – men's department | Orla Kiely | Fendi |
| | Victoria Sleeper Vintage Handbags at Portobello Road Antiques Market | Gucci |
| | Vintage at Rellik | Hermès |
| | | Liberty |
| | | Lulu Guiness |
| | | Prada |
| | | Selfridges |
| | | Stella McCartney |
| | | Vintage from Grays Antique Market |
| | | Vintage from Sotheby's and Christie's auctions, contact the contemporary clothing departments for details of forthcoming sales |
| | | Yves Saint Laurent |
| **Hats and hair accessories** | | |
| Accessorize | By Storm | Gabriella Ligenza |
| John Lewis | Emma Fielden | Harvey Nichols |
| Marks & Spencer | Fenwick | Liberty |
| Woolworths | Kangol | Philip Treacy |
| | Orla Kiely | Rachel Skinner |
| | Rachel Trevor Morgan | Stephen Jones |
| | VV Rouleaux | |
| **Scarves, gloves and belts** | | |
| Accessorize | Aftershock | Etro |
| Gap | Lúki | Gucci |
| John Lewis | Russell & Bromley | Hermès |
| Marks & Spencer | Whistles | Liberty |
| Topshop | | Missoni |
| Vintage from Portobello Road Market | | Prada |
| | | Selfridges |
| **Jewellery** | | |
| Accessorize | Anya | Asprey |
| Diva @ Miss Selfridge | Breil | Boucheron |
| Freedom @ Topshop | Butler & Wilson | Dinny Hall |
| Johnny Loves Rosie | The Cross | Ec One |
| Wallis | Erickson Beamon | Fiona Knapp |
| Vintage from jumble sales | Jewels by Jessy | Garrard |
| | Julie Bloom | Georg Jensen |
| | Kimchi | Pippa Small |
| | Laura Tabor | Tiffany's |
| | Lola Rose | Solange Azagury Partridge |
| | Lúki | Vintage from Gray's Antique Market, and Sotheby's and Christie's Auctions, contact the fine jewellery departments for details of forthcoming sales |
| | Lulu Guinness | |
| | Otazu | |
| | Van Peterson | |
| | Vintage from Portobello Road Market | |
| | Vintage from Merola | |
| | Willma | |
| | Ziio from Fenwick | |

**Shoes & boots**
Birkenstock
Faith
Freeman's
Nine West
Office
Shelly's
Zara

Adidas
Bertie
French Connection
Hobbs
Jigsaw
Karen Millen
LK Bennett
Miu Miu
Nike
Post Mistress
Puma
Russell & Bromley
Wannabee by Patrick Cox

Alberta Ferretti
Jane Brown
Christian Louboutin
Emma Hope
Georgina Goodman
Gina
Gucci
Jimmy Choo
Lambertson Traux
Manolo Blahnik
Mootich
Olivia Morris
Patrick Cox
Paul Smith
Prada
Salvatore Ferragamo
Sergio Rossi
Sigerson Morrison
Stephane Kélian
Yves Saint Laurent

# 07 STORAGE

## £

Argos
B&Q
Homebase
Ikea
Office World

## ££

BoConcept
Cath Kidston
Draks
Driade Storage Systems
Muji
Habitat
The Holding Company
John Lewis
Selfridges

## £££

California Closets
Mobileffe, available at Chaplins
Molteni & Co
Poliform
Purves & Purves
Vistoe

# 08 BEAUTY

## £

**Gowns for red carpet occasions**
Rental from Bodie & Gibbs, Motcomb Street W1
   and other good dress agencies
Designers at Debenhams
Fenn Wright & Manson
Laundry by Shelli Segal
Monsoon
Zara

## ££

Aftershock
Christian Lacroix Bazar
Consortium
Jerome L'Huillier
Kalkarrai
Karen Millen
Ronit Zilkha
Tamarisk

## £££

Alberta Ferretti
Alexander McQueen
Amanda Wakeley
Ben de Lisi
Collette Dinnigan
Dolce & Gabbana
Emanuel Ungaro
Etro
Giorgio Armani
Jenny Packham
John Galliano
Luisa Beccaria
Matches
Missoni
Stella McCartney
Valentino

# 09 HAIR

## Shampoo

**Universal treatments** Shampoo
Daniel Field Spring Water Everyday Shampoo
Dr Hauschka Pure Shampoo
Daniel Field Revitalising Detox Shampoo
Frédéric Fekkai Apple Cider Clarifying Shampoo
Kérastase Specifique Bain Prévention
Louise Galvin Sacred Locks Hair Cleanser
Nirvana Natural Environmental Detox Shampoo
Origins No Deposit Shampoo
Philip Kingsley Moisture Balancing Shampoo
Richard Ward Spring Clean Purifying Detox Shampoo

**Greasy** Shampoo
Darphin Regulating Shampoo with Badian
L'Oréal Professionnel Sebo Control Shampoo
Kérastase Spécifique Bain Divalent – for greasy
   roots and dry ends
Weleda Lemon Balm Shampoo

## Conditioner

**Universal treatments** Conditioner
Daniel Field Revitalising Mineral Conditioner
Dr Hauschka Herbal Hair Conditioner
Frédéric Fekkai Apple Cider Clearing Rinse
Louise Galvin Sacred Locks Hair Moisturiser
Origins Knot Clear Head Mint Rinse
Philip Kingsley Moisture Balancing Conditioner

**Greasy** Conditioner
Weleda Lemon Balm Conditioner

## Treatment/styling

**Universal treatments** Treatment/ styling
Aveda Hair Detoxifier
Daniel Field Smooth & Shine Serum
ghd miracle worker leave-in conditioner
ghd iron styling spray
Louise Galvin Sacred Locks Hair Treatment Masque
Philip Kingsley Elasticizer
Philip Kingsley PM36
Philip Kingsley Moisture Balancing Scalp Tonic
Richard Ward Rescue Me Energising Repair Masque
Richard Ward Fast & Loose Conditioning Mousse
   and Stand & Deliver Ultra Fine Hairspray

**Greasy** Treatment/ styling
Darphin Regulating Complex

**Frizzy** Shampoo
Aveda Sap Moss Shampoo
Daniel Field First Aid Therapy Shampoo
John Frieda Frizz Ease Smooth Start Shampoo
Kérastase Nutritive Bain Oléo-Relax
L'Oréal Professionnel Liss Extrême Shampoo
Philip Kingsley Remoisturising Shampoo
PhytoBrush Shampoo
Richard Ward Rebel Rebel Frizz Control Shampoo

**Frizzy** Conditioner
Aveda Sap Moss Conditioning Detangler
Daniel Field First Aid Conditioner
John Frieda Frizz Ease Gistening Creme
Kérastase Nutritive Masque Oléo-Relax
L'Oréal Professionnel Liss Extrême Conditioner
Philip Kingsley Remoisturising Conditioner
Phyto Défrisant Relaxing Balm
Richard Ward Mane Tame Frizz Control Conditioner

**Frizzy** Treatment/ styling
Aveda Sap Moss Styling Spray
Aveda Hang Straight Straightening Lotion
Bumble and bumble Defrizz
Daniel Field Anti-Frizz Protector Hairspray
ghd indulgence hair beauty mask
John Frieda Frizz Ease Miraculous Recovery
   Conditioning Treatment or Frizz Ease Emergency
   Treatment Leave-in Conditioning Spray
John Frieda Frizz Ease styling range
Kérastase Nutritive Elixir Oléo-Relax
   or Serum Oléo-Relax
Origins Knot Free Finishing Rinse
Philip Kingsley Anti-frizz
Philip Kingsley Remoisturising Scalp Tonic
Phytolisse Smoothing Serum
Richard Ward Sleek Chic Straightening Balm

**Curly** Shampoo
Bumble and bumble Curl Conscious Shampoo
Daniel Field Super-Naturals
   Curl Enhancing Shampoo
Kérastase Nutritive Bain Elasto-Curl
PhytoCurl Shampoo

**Curly** Conditioner
Bumble and bumble Curl Conscious conditioner
Daniel Field Super-Naturals
   Curl Enhancing Conditioner
Kérastase Nutritive Soin Elasto-Curl

**Curly** Treatment/ styling
Aveda Be Curly Curl Enhancing Lotion
Aveda Cherry Almond Bark Conditioning Treatment
Bumble and bumble Curl Creme
Daniel Field Super Naturals Curl Enhancing Spritz
Daniel Field Curl, Hold & Shine
ghd tri style liquid mousse
Kérastase Nutritive Aqua-Mousse Elasto-Curl or
   Crème Elasto-Curl
PhytoCurl Curl Defining Spray

**Fine/ weakened** Shampoo
Bumble and bumble Thickening Shampoo
Daniel Field Body Builder Therapy Shampoo
ghd dead sea mud volumising shampoo
John Frieda Volume Thickening Shampoo
Kérastase Resistance
   Bain de Force or Bain Volumactive
Philip Kingsley Body Building Shampoo
Richard Ward Full On Volume Build Shampoo

**Fine/ weakened** Conditioner
Bumble and bumble Thickening Conditioner
Daniel Field Body Builder Detangling Conditioner
ghd dead sea mud volumising conditioner
John Frieda Volume thickening conditioner
   & strengthening detangler
Kérastase Resistance Forcintense
Kérastase Resistance Ciment Anti-Usure
Kérastase Resistance Vitaliseur
Philip Kingsley Body Building Conditioner

**Fine/ weakened** Treatment/ styling
Aveda Volumizing Tonic
Daniel Field Super Naturals
   Straighten & Smooth Balm
Daniel Field Body Builder Spray
ghd fat hair volumising emulsion
John Frieda Volume Thickening blow dry lotion
Kérastase Resistance Expanseur Extra-Corps
   or Mousse Volumactive
Philip B Rejuvenating Oil
Philip Kingsley Maximiser
Philip Kingsley Body Building Scalp Tonic
Richard Ward High & Mighty Root Boost
   Thickening Spray

**Dry/ brittle** Shampoo
Aveda Curessence Damage Relief Shampoo
Daniel Field Plant Remoisturising Shampoo
ghd intensive care treatment shampoo
Kérastase Nutritive Bain Satin 1, 2 or 3
Origins The Last Straw Conditioning Shampoo
Richard Ward Crowning Glory
   Moisture Rich Shampoo
Weleda Rosemary Shampoo

**Dry/ brittle** Conditioner
Aveda Curessence Damage Relief Conditioner
Daniel Field Plant Remoisturising Treatment
ghd intensive care treatment conditioner
Kérastase Nutritive Lait Vital or Aqua-Oleum
Kérastase Nutritive Masquintense Cheveaux
Origins Happy Endings Conditioner
Richard Ward Glory Restorer
   Moisture Surge Conditioner
Weleda Rosemary Conditioner

**Dry/ brittle** Treatment/styling
Aveda Brilliant Damage Control
Aveda Deep Penetrating Hair Revitalizer
Daniel Field Smooth & Shine Serum
ghd halo non silicone serum
Frédéric Fekkai glossing cream
Kérastase Nutritive Nutri-Sculpt range
The Organic Pharmacy Hair Serum
Origins Rich Rewards Intensive Moisture Treatment
Phytokarité Intensive Treatment Mask
Weleda Rosemary Hair Lotion

**Dandruff & flaky scalp** Shampoo
Barefoot Botanicals
   SOS Hair & Scalp Rescue shampoo
Daniel Field Dandruff Scalp Therapy Shampoo
Darphin Anti-dandruff shampoo with Sage
ghd invigoration shampoo
Kérastase Spécifique Gommage Cheveux Secs
Kérastase Bain Vital Haute Tolérance
   or Bain Riche Haute Tolérance
Nirvana Natural White Nettle & Thyme Shampoo
Nizoral A-D shampoo
Philip Kingsley Flaky Itchy Scalps Shampoo
PhytoRetard – for severe & oily dandruff
PhytoLithol – for sensitive & itchy dandruff
PhytoSylic – for flaky scalp

**Dandruff & flaky scalp** Conditioner
Barefoot Botanicals
   SOS Hair & Scalp Rescue conditioner
ghd invigoration conditioner

**Dandruff & flaky scalp** Treatment/ styling
For flaky scalp, rinse with organic cider vinegar
Aveda Scalp Remedy Anti-dandruff Tonic
Dr Hauschka Neem Hair Lotion
Kérastase Noctocalm night serum
The Organic Pharmacy Nourishing Hair & Scalp Oil
Philip Kingsley Intensive Anti Dandruff Treatment
Philip Kingsley Flaky Itchy Scalp Tonic
PhytoSquame treatment

**Maintaining coloured hair** Shampoo
Aveda Color Conserve Shampoo
Aveda Color Enhancer shampoos
Bumble and bumble color support shampoos
Frédéric Fekkai Red Shampoo
   and Brown Shampoo
Frédéric Fekkai Baby Blonde Shampoo
John Frieda Brilliant Brunette Shampoo
   and Sheer Blonde Highlight Activating Shampoo
L'Oreal Professionnel
   Vitamino Color Protective Shampoo
Philip B White Truffle Moisturising Shampoo
Phytocitrus Shine Shampoo
Richard Ward Guardian Angel Colour Protect
   Shampoo

**Maintaining coloured hair** Conditioner
Aveda Color Conserve Conditioner
Aveda Color Enhancer Conditioners
Bumble and bumble Color Support Conditioners
Frédéric Fekkai Baby Blonde Conditioner
John Frieda Brilliant Brunette Conditioner or Sheer
   Blonde Instant Conditioner and Highlight
   Enhancer
L'Oreal Professionnel
   Vitamino Color Protective Conditioner
Richard Ward True Colours
   Colour Protect Conditioner

**Maintaining coloured hair** Treatment/ styling
Frédéric Fekkai Baby Blonde Hair Treatment
ghd angel tears
ghd iron oil
John Frieda Brilliant Brunette styling range
John Frieda Sheer Blonde Hair Repair
John Frieda Sheer Blonde styling range
Phytocitrus Essential Nutrition Mask

**Thinning hair** Shampoo
Phytocyane thinning hair treatment shampoo

**Thinning hair** Treatment/ styling
Darphin Revitalising Complex
Philip Kingsley Intensive Scalp Treatment
Phytocyane thinning hair treatment ampoules

**Sun and swimming** Shampoo
John Frieda Beach Blonde
    Cool Dip Refreshing Shampoo
ghd sun survivor shampoo
ghd pure detox shampoo
Kérastase Soleil Bain Après Soleil
UltraSwim Protective Shampoo

**Sun and swimming** Conditioner
ghd sun survivor conditioner
John Frieda Beach Blonde
    Cool Dip Detangling Conditioner
Kérastase Soleil Crème Richesse
UltraSwim Protective Conditioner

**Sun and swimming** Treatment/ styling
ghd sun worshipper
ghd cooling mist
John Frieda Beach Blonde Life Preserver
    hair conditioning oil
John FriedaBeach Blonde Gold Rush shimmer gel
John Frieda Beach Blonde Lemon Lights
John Frieda Sun Streaks heat-accelerated
    highlighter
Kérastase Soleil Lait Après-Soleil
    & Aqua Protective
Philip Kingsley Swimcap
Philip Kingsley Weatherproof sun spray

**Styling Tools**
Babyliss Curling Tongs
Carmen Heated Rollers
Comby velcro rollers
ghd original ceramic styling irons
    & ghd mini styler
Parlux Professional Hairdryers

# 10 MAKE-UP

| £ | ££ | £££ |
|---|---|---|
| **Preparing Your Skin** | | |
| **20s – 30s** | | |
| Barbara Daly for Tesco Radiant Touch Skin Illuminator & Make-up Transformer | NARS Make-up Primer | Darphin Aromatic Purifying Balm |
| | Lancôme Illuminator | DDF Bio Active Nourishing Serum |
| | Chanel Illuminating Make-up Base | DDF Cellular Repair Moisturizer |
| | Clarins Beauty Flash Balm | |
| | Delux Beauty at Pout | |
| |   Liquid Pearl Luminizer Lotion for Face & Body | |
| | Origins A Perfect World White Tea Skin Guardian | |
| **40s – 50s** | | |
| Revlon Skinlights Face Illuminator | Estée Lauder Perfectionist | Dr Sebagh Deep Exfoliating Mask |
| |   Correcting Serum for Lines/ Wrinkles | Guerlain Issima Midnight Star |
| | Magic by Prescriptives Illuminating Liquid Potion |   Extraordinary Radiance Treatment |
| | Origins Out Smart Face Protector SPF25 | SK-II Facial Treatment Essence |
| | MAC Strobe Cream | Jan Marini C'Esta Serum |
| **60+** | | |
| Drink plenty of water. As you get older your skin gets drier. You really need the hydration. | Estée Lauder Spotlight Skin Tone Perfector | La Prairie Cellular Treatment |
| Oenobiol Anti-Age Supplement | Laura Mercier Secret Brightener |   Rose Illusion Line Filler |
| Body Shop Shimmer and Glow | Red Earth Corrective Make-up Base | Jan Marini Age Intervention Face Cream |
|   face and body lotion | Elizabeth Arden Let There be Light | Lancôme Cream Absolute |
| |   Radiant Skin Lotion | |
| | Red Earth Moisturising Make-up base | |
| | Origins Grin from Year to Year | |
| |   Brightening face firmer | |
| **Brows** | | |
| Body Shop Eyebrow Make-up | Cargo Eye Shadow in Columbia | Laura Mercier Brow Powder duo |
| Tesco Nail Scissors | Space NK Brow Brush | Tweezerman Slant Tweezer |
| Bourjois Eyeshadow in Brun Gris | Shu Uemura Eyebrow Manicure | Talika Eyebrow Extender |
| Rimmel Special Eyes Mono | MAC Stud Eyebrows Crayon | Chanel Brow Compact |
|   in Dusk or Smoky Quartz | MAC 266 Brush | |
| | Paula Dorf Brow Duo | |
| | Shiseido Brow Gel | |
| | Shavata eyebrow shapers | |
| | Laura Mercier eyebrow pencil | |
| **Skin** | | |
| **20s – 30s** | | |
| Barbara Daly for Tesco Moisture Foundation | Laura Mercier Moisturising foundation | Chantecaille Real Skin |
| Barbara Daly for Tesco Ultra Light Pressed Powder | Lancôme Transparence de Teint | |
| Revlon Skinlights Custom Face Powders | Shu Uemura Face Powder | |
| | Estée Lauder Lucidity Translucent loose powder | |
| | Chanel Teint Universal Foundation | |
| **40s – 50s** | | |
| Barbara Daly for Tesco Oil-free Foundation | Laura Mercier Oil-Free Foundation | Chantecaille Future Skin oil-free gel foundation |
| Bourjois Comme L'air Loose Powder | Becca Fine Loose Finishing Powder | La Prairie Skin Caviar |
| Barbara Daly for Tesco | Trish McEvoy Even Skin Foundation | |
|   Ultra Light Translucent Powder | Chanel Teint Compact Universal Foundation | |

**60+**

| | | |
|---|---|---|
| Revlon Skinlights Illusion Wand flaw-diffusing concealer | Prescriptives Traceless Skin Responsive Tint | Vincent Longo Water Canvas Creme-to-Powder Foundation |
| Maybelline Wonder Finish Make-up Liquid to Powder foundation | Laura Mercier Tinted Moisturiser SPF20 | Chantecaille Real Skin translucent make-up |
| Barbara Daly for Tesco Face Lift make-up | NARS Face Glow | Guerlain Météorites Voyage Compact Powder |
| | Chanel Vitalumiere Foundation | Lancôme Palette Mix |
| | Lancôme Photogenic Ultra Confort Light Reflecting Make-up | |

**Concealers** Spots

| | | |
|---|---|---|
| Barbara Daly for Tesco concealer | Vincent Longo Creme Concealer | Laura Mercier Secret Camouflage |
| Maybelline EverFresh Concealer | Paula Dorf Total Camouflage | Chantecaille Total Concealer |
| | Benefit Boi-ing | |

**Concealers** Dark circles

| | | |
|---|---|---|
| Revlon Skinlights Illusion Wand | Stephane Marais Perfect Concealer | YSL Touche Eclat |
| Barbara Daly for Tesco Luminous Eye Care | Estée Lauder Disappear Smoothing Creme Concealer | Laura Mercier Secret Concealer & Powder |
| Bourjois Light Reflecting Concealer | Prescriptives Traceless Skin Responsive Corrector | Laura Mercier Secret Brightener |
| | Benefit Ooh La Lift | |
| | Prescriptives Traceless Skin Responsive Corrector | |

**Concealer** Blemishes/pigment

| | | |
|---|---|---|
| Barbara Daly for Tesco True Skin | Prescriptives Traceless Skin Responsive Corrector | Trish McEvoy Even Skin Extra Coverage Concealer |
| | Estée Lauder Disappear Smoothing Creme Concealer | |
| | Derma Color Camouflage System Tester Kit (includes Camouflage cream in 7 shades, fixing powder, cleansing cream, moisturizer cream, cleansing lotion, cleansing milk and make-up remover) | |
| | DermaColor Camouflage Make-up mini-palette | |

**Cheeks** Dry/hairy

| | | |
|---|---|---|
| Revlon Skinlights Color Lighting for eyes/ cheeks | MAC Tint Frost Cream Colour Base | Chanel Face Stick |
| | MAC Premeditated Cream Cream Colour Base | Stila Rose Convertible Colour |
| | Delux Beauty Gel Stick | Chantecaille Aqua Blush |
| | Delux Beauty Face Shine | NARS Multiple Stick |
| | Lancôme Colour Dose Lips and Cheeks | |
| | NARS Cream Blush | |
| | Spa.NK Cheek Tint | |
| | Trish McEvoy Model's Choice cream blusher | |
| | Origins Pinch Your Cheeks | |

**Cheeks** Oily/flawed/scarred

| | | |
|---|---|---|
| Barbara Daly for Tesco Powder Blush | Estée Lauder Blushing Natural Cheek Color | Chanel Irreelle Blush |
| Bourjois Powder Blush | NARS Powder Blush | RMK Powder Blush |
| Lancôme Blush Papier Nacré | MAC Powder Blush | |
| | MAC Sheer Tones Blusher | |
| | Yves Saint Laurent Touche Blush | |

**Lips** Thin

| | | |
|---|---|---|
| Barbara Daly for Tesco Lip Pencil | Pout Lipslick | Chantecaille Lip Gloss |
| L'Oreal Glam Shine | Benefit Benetint | Chanel Gossimer |
| Lancôme Juicy Tubes | DuWop Lip Venom | Chanel Levres Scilliant |
| | Benefit Lip Plump | |
| | Yves Saint Laurent Lisse Gloss | |
| | Shu Uemura Sweet Lip Gloss | |
| | Pout Lip Gloss | |
| | Elizabeth Arden High Shine Lip Gloss | |

**Lips** Lined

| | | |
|---|---|---|
| Barbara Daly for Tesco Luminous Lip Care | Estée Lauder Pure Color Lip Gloss | Guerlain Divinora Lip Lift Beautifying Fixative |
| Barbara's Private Collection Lip Pumice | MAC Tinted Lip Conditioner | Elizabeth Arden Lip Fix Cream |
| Max Factor Lipfinity Everlites | Origins Bite Your Lips | Magic by Prescriptives Invisible Line Smoother |
| | Paula Dorf Perfect Illusion Lipline Filler | |
| | Red Earth Lip Tint Compact | |
| | Space NK Lip Colour | |
| | Space NK Lip Gloss | |

**Lips** Dry

| | | |
|---|---|---|
| Carmex | Origins Lip Remedy | Creme de la Mer The Lip Balm |
| Revlon Skinlights lip colour | Laura Mercier Lip Silk | Elizabeth Arden Eight Hour Cream |
| Barbara's Private Collection Lipstick | Lancôme Juicy Tubes | Stila Lip Glaze |
| L'Oreal Pastel Repair Shimmery Conditioning Lip Cream | Smith's Rosebud Salve | Benefit Dr Feelgood Lipscription |
| L'Oreal Pastel Repair Conditioning Lip Cream | Shu Uemura Sweet Lip Gloss | NARS Lip Lacquer |
| | Elizabeth Arden Eight Hour Cream Lip Protectant Stick | |
| | MAC Tinted Lip Conditioner | |
| | Dr Haushka Lip Care Stick | |
| | Benefit Benetint Lip Balm | |
| | Pout Lip Gloss | |

**Lips** Uneven

| | | |
|---|---|---|
| Barbara Daly for Tesco Liquid Lips | Estée Lauder Pure Colour Gloss | Chanel Lip Liner Crayon Pour les Levres |
| Barbara Daly for Tesco Lip Gloss | MAC Spice Lip Pencil | Stila Lip Gloss |
| Max Factor Lip Liner | RMK Lip Liner pencil | Stila Lip Polish |

**Eyes** Hooded
Eylure individual lashes
Bourjois Liquid Liner in plum
Bourjois Eyeshadow Gris Magnetique
Bourjois Coup de Theatre Mascara

Shu Uemura Eyelash Curler
Lancôme Ampercils Waterproof Mascara
NARS Eyeliner Pencil
Hard Candy Eyeliner
Laura Mercier Long Wear Eye Pencil
Cargo Powder Eyeshadow in Columbia
Stila Powder Shadow in Storm
Kiss Me Mascara

ModelCo Lash Wand heated eyelash curler
Yves Saint Laurent False Lash Effect Mascara
Stila Eye Glaze Cream Shadow

**Eyes** Deepset
Bourjois Triple Eyeshadow
Bourjois Effet Lumiere Eye Shadow
Bourjois Eyeliner Pencil
Maybelline Cool Effect Shadow/ Liner Pencil
L'Oreal Lash Architect Mascara

Lancôme Colour Dose Eyes
NARS Eyeshadow in All About Eve
Pout Miss Tahiti Eye Shadow
Estée Lauder MagnaScopic Mascara
NARS Eyeshadow in Blonde
Spa.NK Waterproof Mascara

Stila Eye Glaze Cream Shadow
Chanel Crayon pour les Yeux
Chanel Ombre Unique Cream
ModelCo Lash Wand Heated Eyelash Curler

**Eyes** Lined
Maybelline Great Lash Mascara
Barbara Daly for Tesco Easy on the Eye Pencil
Tesco eyelash curlers
Barbara Daly for Tesco Eye Base
Eye Dew Clear eye drops
Revlon Eyeglide Shimmer Shadow

Origins Underwear for Lids
Delux Beauty Cream Base
Stila Smudge Pots
Laura Mercier Eye Basics

Magic by Prescriptives Invisible Line Smoother

**Nails**
Nails Inc. Wonder Oil range
Mavala Nail Polish in brights
Body Shop nail buffer
Body Shop sweet almond oil

Aveda Cuticle Control
Bloom Nail Polish
Bloom Cuticle Quencher
Essie Nail Colours
Opi Nail Colours and Diamond Top Coat
Jessica Nail Colour
Estée Lauder Pure Colour Nail Gloss
Dr Hauschka Neem Nail Oil Pen
Nails Inc. Downing Street Diamonds hardening
    base coat
Nails Inc. Soho Silk liquid wrap
The Organic Pharmacy Neem and Lemon Nail Oil
Nailtiques Nail Protein and Nail Treatments

Clarins Crème Jeunesse des Mains
Guerlain Issima anti-ageing hand care
Jan Marini Age Intervention Hands
Nails Inc. Everlasting Polish treatment
The Organic Pharmacy Rose
    herbal hand and nail balm
Talika Instant Manicure,
    whitening and coating oxygen treatment

**How to keep make-up fresh all day**
Body Shop Lip Line Fixer
Smith's Rosebud Salve from Mister Mascara

Barbara's Private Collection Mineral Mist
Benefit Dr Feelgood invisible refiner
Benefit Ooh La Lift
Clinique Stay-matte oil blotting sheets
ModelCo make-up remover
    cotton buds – available at Space NK
Laura Mercier Secret Finish

Crème de la Mer The Mist
Stila Mini Brush set
Guerlain Happology Eye Cream

# 11 TRAVELLING

## £

**Clothing**
Esprit
Etam
Gap
John Lewis
Knickerbox
Mango
New Look
Oasis
Pineapple
Portobello Road Market
Primark
Zara

## ££

Adidas
Billabong
Diesel
French Connection
Fuertaventura @ Sweaty Betty
Ghost
John Smedley
Miss Sixty
Nuala by Puma
Puma
Rokit
Royal Elastics
Sand
Seal Kay
Sweaty Betty

## £££

Calvin Klein
Fake London
Firetrap
Maharishi
Marc by Marc Jacobs
Matches stores
SportMax
Prada Sport

**Luggage & travel bags**
Delsey
John Lewis
Marks & Spencer
Textier
Woolworths

Brics
Cath Kidston
Helen Kaminski @ Heidi Klein
Lúki
Orla Kiely
Rodeo Star @ Harvey Nichols
Samsonite
Swiss Army

Bill Amberg
Burberry's
Fendi
Gucci
Hermès
J&M Davidson
Louis Vuitton
Mandarina Duck
Mulberry
Prada
Tumi

**Swimwear**
6ixty 8ight @ figleaves.com
Debenhams
Dorothy Perkins
George at Asda
John Lewis
H&M
Knickerbox
Marks & Spencer
Miss Selfridge
Topshop
Warehouse

Calvin Klein
Exotica of Brazil
French Connection
Huit
Mambo
Pink Piranha
Sea Folly
Speedo

Cacharel
Celine
Escada Sport
Gucci
Heidi Klein @ Heidi Klein
La Perla
Liza Bruce
Marlies Dekker
Matches
Melissa Odabash @ Heidi Klein
Missoni

**Sunglasses**
H&M
Spitfire, available at Topshop
Woolworth's
Zara

Boots the Chemist
Calvin Klein Eyewear
Diesel Sunglasses
Miu Miu
Ray-Ban
Sunglasses Hut

Alain Mikli
Boucheron
Chanel
Chloé Lunettes
Costume National Eyewear
Cutler & Gross, contemporary & vintage
Dior
Dolce & Gabbana Eyewear
Gucci
Missoni
Oliver Peoples
Persol
Prada
Stella McCartney
Valentino
YSL

**Remedies**
Ainsworth's Homeopathic Pharmacy for
   homeopathic jet-lag pills
Air Flight Gel
Aveda Peppymint breath freshener
Bach Flower Remedies: Rescue Remedy
Dr Hauschka Fitness Leg Spray
Emergen-C vitamin sachet from Fresh & Wild
ESPA Lifelines roller oils
Helios Homeopathics Homeopathy Specifics kit –
   36 Remedies for the Traveller
Human Nature Energy Bomb
The Organic Pharmacy In-flight kit
Origins Peace of Mind pump
Quest Evening Primrose oil
Tisserand Tea Tree & Kanuka Blemish Stick
Tisserand Citronella oil to repel mosquitoes

**Toiletries**
Capsule Collection available at Debenhams
Dr Hauschka Firming Face Mask
Guerlain Eye Balm
Guerlain Midnight Secret
Human Nature Soapoo, two in one
Jo Malone In-Flight bag – full of Jo Malone
   goodies, luxury!
La Mer Mist by Crème de la Mer
Lancaster mini sun cream
Lancôme mini mascara
Muji plastic bottles and decanters
Philip Kingsley hair products in trial sizes
Richard Ward 'Mini Me's' travel size hair products
Swab Plus liquid-filled cotton buds, includes eye
   make-up remover, Vitamin E lip care, nail polish
   remover, cuticle treatment
Talika eye decompress
Trish McEvoy mini compact and brush set

**Comfort**
Ballantyne Cashmere
Boots the Chemist earplugs
Bose noise reduction headphones
Brora
Portobello Cashmere Shop
Pringle

# 12 PREGNANCY
## Remedies & beauty products

Caudalie Huile Energie & Fermete
Environ Proactive Intensive Hydrating Oil
Ionithermie Bust Treatment
Thermal clay and algae firming treatment
Natalia Prenatal anti-stretch oil
Natalia Prenatal leg refresher gel
Natalia Prenatal relax and soothe kit

The Organic Pharmacy
   Labour and Post Labour kit
The Organic Pharmacy Miracle Nipple Cream
Phytomer SeaTonic Toning Bust Gel
Phytomer SeaTonic Stretch Mark Reducing Cream
Simulcium G3 available from
   the French Cosmetic Medical Company

Sisley Phytobuste
   Intensive Bust Cream
Sisley Phytobuste
   Intensive Bust Compound
Thalgo Stretch Mark Cream
Thalgo Bust Shaping Serum

**£**

**£££**

**£££**

**Clothing**
Accessorize – great sarongs
Gap Body
H&M – for cheaper trendy moment
Knickerbox – sleeveless T shirts
Mango – great for inexpensive jumpers that you
   won't mind stretching
Zara TRF

Blossom Mother & Child
Citizens of Humanity – jeans
Earl Jean
Elle Macpherson Maternelle – underwear
For All Mankind – jeans
Fuertaventura, available at Sweaty Betty
Issa, available at Blossom Mother &Child
Juicy Jeans
Liz Lange available at 9 London
   and Serendipity-online.com
Michael Stars – T-shirts
Nuala for Puma
Toller – easy day wear,
   available at Blossom Mother & Child

Allegra Hicks – kaftan tops
Chaiken evening wear – available at 9 London
Clements Ribeiro
Diane von Furstenberg – her stretchy wrap styles
   are ideal for the bump. Available at 9 London
Gharani Strok
Maria Grachvogel
Marilyn Moore
Megan Park
Matthew Williamson
Temperley – available at Blossom Mother & Child

# S&T'S ADDRESS BOOK

**6ixty Eight** available at www.figleaves.com
**9 London** 020 7352 7600
**? Air** SW13 020 8741 0816,
SE21 020 8288 4252, NW3 020 7435 9221,
W11 020 7221 8163, SW19 020 8879 0366
**The Abbey** 020 8772 6674
**Accessorize**
0870 412 9000 www.accessorize.co.uk
**Adidas** 0870 240 4204 www.adidas.co.uk
**Affleck's Palace** 0161 834 2039
www.afflecks-palace.co.uk
**Aftershock** 020 8963 8500
**Agatha** 020 7495 2779
**Age Concern** 0800 00 99 66
**Agent Provocateur**
020 7927 6999 www.agentprovocateur.com
**Ainsworth's Homeopathic Pharmacy**
020 7486 4313 www.ainsworths.com
**Air Flight Gel** 020 7328 5452
**Alain Mikli** 0800 0569 067 www.mikli.fr
**A la Mode** 020 7730 7180
**Alberta Ferretti**
020 7235 2349 www.albertaferretti.com
**Alexander McQueen**
020 7278 4333 www.alexandermcqueen.com
**All Aboard** 020 8381 1717
**Allegra Hicks** 020 7235 8989
**Amanda Wakeley** 020 7590 9105,
www.amandawakeley.co.uk
**Anna** Bury St Edmunds 01284 706 944, King's
Lynn 01328 730 325, London 020 7483 0411
**Ann-Louise Roswald** 020 7250 1583
**Anya** www.anyalondon.com
**Anya Hindmarch** 020 7838 9177
www.anyahindmarch.com
**Argos** www.argos.co.uk
**Aristoc** 01623 444 299
**Arkangel** 0131 226 4466
**Armstrong's** 0131 220 5557
**Asda** 0500 100 055
**Asprey** 020 7493 6767
**Aubade** 01327 811 289
**Aveda** 01730 232 380
**Aurora Photo Rejuvenation IPL**
available at Dr Jean-Louis Sebagh
020 7637 0548 and good cosmetic surgeons

**Babyliss Curling Tongs** 0870 513 3191
www.babyliss.co.uk
**Bach's Flower Remedies** 020 7495 2404
www.bachessences.com
**Balenciaga** available at Selfridges, Harvey
Nichols, Browns, Joseph and selected boutiques,
www.balenciaga.com
**Ballantyne Cashmere**
available at Brown's, Harrods, Harvey Nichols &
Liberty. www.ballantyne.it
**Barbara Daly for Tesco** 0800 505 555
**Barbara's Private Collection** 01279 814 365
**Barefoot Botanicals** 0870 220 2273
**Barnardo's** 08457 69 79 67
**Beauty Tools** available at Sally Hair & Beauty
Supplies 020 7434 0064
**Becca Cosmetics**
available at Space NK 020 7299 4999
**Ben de Lisi** 020 7730 2994
www.bendelisi.com
**Benefit** 0901 113 0001

**Benetton** 020 7389 8124 www.benetton.com
**Bernard's** 01372 468 032
**Bertie** 020 7380 3800
**Betsey Johnson** 020 7591 0005
**Betty Jackson**
020 7589 7884 www.bettyjackson.com
**Billabong** www.billabong.com
**Bill Amberg**
020 8960 2000 www.billamberg.com
**Billy Bag**
available at Selfridges 0870 837 7377
**Birkenstock** The Boot Tree 020 7602 2866
**Birkenstock** The Natural Shoe Store
0800 132 194 www.birkenstock.co.uk
**Bliss** 020 8969 3331
**Bloom** available at Pout 020 7379 0379
www.pout.co.uk
**Blossom Mother & Child** 020 7589 7500
www.blossommotherandchild.com
**Blue Lawn** 01245 250 083
**Blue Rinse** 0113 245 1735
**Blumarine** 020 7493 4872
available at Harvey Nichols 020 7235 5000
**BoConcept** www.boconcept.com
**Bodas** 020 7792 4915 www.bodas.co.uk
**Bodie & Gibbs** 020 7259 6620
**The Body Shop**
01903 844 554 www.thebodyshop.com
**Boots the Chemist**
08450 70 80 90 www.boots.com
**Bose** www.bose.co.uk
**Boucheron** www.boucheron.com
**Boucheron Sunglasses** 01483 302 882
**Bourjois** 0800 269 836
**B&Q** www.diy.com
**Brava Bra** from The Harley Medical Group
0800 085 9085 www.mybrava.org.uk
**Bravissimo** www.bravissimo.com
**Breil** 01628 77 09 88
**Brics** 020 8731 3500
**Brite Smile** UK 08707 800 901
www.britesmile.co.uk
**British Heart Foundation shops**
0870 120 4141
**British Red Cross** www.redcross.org.uk
**Brora** 020 7736 9944 www.brora.co.uk
**Brown's** 020 7514 0000
**Brown Thomas** 00 353 1605 6666
**Bumble and bumble** 01768 895 505
**Burberry's** 020 7968 0192
**Butler & Wilson** 020 7409 2955
www.butlerandwilson.co.uk
**By Storm** 020 7224 7888
www.bystorm.co.uk

**Cacharel** 020 7383 3000
**California Closets** 020 8208 4544
**Calvin Klein Eyewear** 0800 722 020
**Calvin Klein Underwear & Swimwear**
available at Selfridges 08708 377 377
**Cancer Research UK shops** 01403 210585
www.cancerresearchuk.org/getinvolved/shops/shops/
**Capsule Collection**
available at Debenhams 020 7408 4444
**Cargo** available at Pout 020 7379 0379
www.pout.co.uk
**Carmen Heated Rollers** 0161 947 3000
**Carmex** available at pharmacists nationwide

**Cath Kidston**
020 7229 8000 www.cathkidston.co.uk
**Catherine Barclay** 01603 626 751
**Catherine Walker** 020 7352 4626
**Caudalie** 020 7304 7038
**Céline** 020 7279 4999
**Chaiken** available at 9 London 020 7352 7600
**Chanel Cosmetics** 020 7493 3836
**Chanel Boutique** 020 7493 5040
www.chanel.com
**Chanel Sunglasses** 020 7493 3836
**The Changing Room** 01892 547899
**Chantecaille** (at Fenwick) 020 7629 9161
**Chaplins** www.chaplins.co.uk
**Chattertons** 01494 722 894
**Chloé** 020 7823 5348
available at Harvey Nichols 020 7235 5000
**Chloé Lunettes** 01635 277 299
**Choice** 01708 742 231
**Christian Lacroix Bazar**
**Christian Louboutin** 020 7823 2234
**Christie's Auctions** 020 7581 7611
**Citizens of Humanity**
**Clarins** 0800 036 3558
**Clements Ribeiro**
available at Selfridges and www.netaporter.com
**Clinique** 01730 232 566
**The Clothes Room** 01423 889 090
**Club** 020 7235 2242
**Coccinelle** 020 7491 7414
**Cochinechine** 020 7435 9377
**Coco Ribbon** 020 7727 6760
**Colgate Fluoride Toothpaste**
available at pharmacies nationwide
**Collette Dinnigan** 020 7589 8897
**Comby velcro rollers** available from
Sally Hair & Beauty Supplies 020 7434 0064
**Consortium** 020 7631 1628
**Corniche** 0131 556 3707
**Cornucopia** 020 7828 5752
**Costume National Eyewear** 01635 277 277
**The Courtyard** 01483 452 825
**Crème de la Mer** 01730 232 566
**Cricket** 0151 227 4645
**The Cross** 020 7727 6760
**Cruise** Edinburgh 0131 220 4441, Glasgow
0141 572 3232, Newcastle 0191 261 0510
**Cutler & Gross**
contemporary: 020 7581 2250,
vintage: 020 7590 9995

**Damaris** 020 7963 2000
**D&G** 020 7878 8600
**Daniel Field** 0845 230 2124
**Daniel Galvin Salon** 020 7486 8601
**Darphin** 020 8847 1777
**DDF** available at Harvey Nichols 020 7235 5000
**Debenhams**
020 7408 4444 www.debenhams.com
**Decleor** 020 7402 9474
**Delsey** 020 8731 3530
**Delux Beauty** available at Pout 020 7379 0379
www.pout.co.uk
**Dentics** 07000 336 842 www.dentics.co.uk
**Derma Color** available at Screenface
020 7221 8289 www.screenface.com
**Designers at Debenhams**
020 7408 4444 www.debenhams.com

**Diane von Furstenberg**
020 7221 1120 www.dvflondon.com
**Diesel** 020 7833 2255 www.diesel.com
**Diesel Sunglasses** 020 7841 5999
**Dinny Hall** 020 7792 3913 www.dinnyhall.com
**Dior Sunglasses** 020 7841 5999
**Diva** 01277 844 156, available at Miss Selfridge
**Diverse** 020 7359 8877
**Dr Hauschka and Dr Hauschka Estheticians**
01386 792 642 www.drhauschka.co.uk
**Dr Sebagh** 020 7637 0548 www.drsebagh.com
**Dolce & Gabbana** 020 7659 9000
**Dolce & Gabbana Eyewear** 01635 277 277
**Dorothy Perkins** 0800 731 8285
**Doyle's** 01858 463 409
**Driade Storage Systems** available at Selfridges
0870 837 7377 www.driade.com
**Draks** 01869 232 989
**Dries Van Noten**
available at Selfridges and Harvey Nichols
**Dstress** 020 7727 0490 www.dstressdirect.com
**DuWop** available at Pout 020 7379 0379
www.pout.co.uk

**Earl Jean** 020 7727 9902
**East Street** 01798 344 165
**Ec One** 020 7243 8811
**Elizabeth Arden**
020 7574 2722 www.elizabetharden.com
**Elizabeth Kompala's Problem Skin lotion**
available from Human Nature 020 7328 5452
**Elle Macpherson Intimates** 020 7478 0280
**Elspeth Gibson**
020 7235 0601 www.elspethgibson.com
**Emanuel Ungaro** 020 7629 0550
**Emergen-C** sachets available at chemists
and health food stores nationwide
**Emilio Pucci** 020 7201 8171
**Emma Fielden** 020 8509 8479
**Emma Hope** 020 7259 9566
**Endermologie**
for salon locations 020 8731 5678
**Environ @ Fiona & Marie Facial Aesthetics**
020 7908 3773 www.environ.co.za
**Eporex** available at Pasha Clinic 020 7409 7354
**Erickson Beamon** 020 7259 0202
**Escada & Escada Sport** 020 7580 6066
**ESPA** 01252 742 800 www.espaonline.com
**Esprit** 020 7025 7707
**Essie** 020 8906 9090 www.nailsbymail.co.uk
**Estée Lauder** 01730 232 566
**Esthederm** available at Space NK 020 7229 4999
**Etam** 020 7494 7400
**Etro** 020 7495 5767 www.etro.it
**Eve Lom** available at Space NK 020 7229 4999
**Exotica of Brazil** 020 7835 0669 www.exotica.co.uk
**Eye Dew** available at pharmacists nationwide
**Eyesential** 0870 4202942
**Eylure** available at Boots the Chemist
08450 70 80 90 www.boots.com

**Faith** 0800 289 297
**Fake London** 020 7287 6767
**Falke** 020 7493 8442
**Fantasie** 01536 764 337
**Fantasy Tan** 0870 240 7072
**Feathers** 020 7243 8800

**Fendi** 020 7838 6288 www.fendi.com
**Fenn Wright & Manson**
020 7323 4821
www.fennwrightmanson.com
**Fenwick** 020 7629 9161
**Figleaves.com** www.figleaves.com
**Fiona Knapp** 020 7313 5941
**Fiona & Marie Aesthetics** 020 7908 3773
**Firetrap** 020 8753 0280 www.firetrap.net
**Flannels** Birmingham 0121 633 4154, Manchester
0161 832 5536, Nottingham 0115 947 6466
**Fogal** 020 7235 3115 www.fogal.com
**Footlights** 01932 860 190
**For All Mankind**
available at Harvey Nichols 020 7235 5000
**Frédéric Fekkai**
available at Space NK 020 7299 4999
**Freedom @ Topshop** 01277 844 186
**Freeman's** 020 7820 2000
**French Connection** 020 7399 7200
**French Cosmetic Medical Company**
020 7637 0548
**Fresh & Wild** 0800 917 5175
**Freya** 01536 764 337
**Frock Brokers** 020 7538 0370
**FrostFrench** 020 7267 9991
**Frownies** 01273 703 461
**Fuertaventura** available at Sweaty Betty
0800 169 3889 www.sweatybetty.com
**Furla** 020 7629 9827 www.furla.com
**Futur-Tec** 020 7431 1033

**Gabriella Ligenza** 020 7730 2200
**Gant** 08451 11 10 10 www.gant.com
**Gap & Gap Body** 0800 427 789
**Garbo** Wilmslow 01625 521 212,
Wigan 01257 426 995, Southport 01704 544 430
**Garnier Ambre Solaire** 0845 399 0404
**Garrard** 0870 871 8888
**Gatineau** 0800 731 5805
**Genevieve** 020 8458 9616
**Georg Jensen** 020 7499 6541
www.georgjensen.com
**George at Asda** 0500 100 055
**Georges Rech** 01753 869 990
**Georgina Goodman** 020 7499 8599
www.georginagoodman.com
**Gerbe** available at Selfridges 0870 837 7377
**Gharani Strok** 020 8749 5909
www.gharanistrok.co.uk
**ghd haircare & ceramic styling irons**
0845 330 1133 www.ghdhair.com
**Ghost** 020 8960 3121 www.ghost.co.uk
**Gillette Venus** www.gillettevenus.com
**Gina** 020 7235 2932 www.ginashoes.com
**Giorgio Armani**
020 7235 6232 www.giorgioarmani.com
**Giulio** 01223 423 776
**Givenchy Couture**
available at Harrods 020 7730 1234
**Givenchy Beauty** 020 7563 8800
**Goddess** 01536 764 337
**Gossard** 01525 859 760
**Gray's Antique Market** 020 7629 7034
**Gucci** 020 7629 2716 www.gucci.com
**Gucci Sunglasses** 020 7841 5999
**Guerlain** 01932 233 874
www.guerlain.com

**Habitat** www.habitat.co.uk
**H&M** 020 7323 2211
**Hambledon** 01962 890 055
**Hannah Lee** 020 7586 4121
**Hanro** www.hanro.com
available at Fenwick 020 7629 9161
**Hard Candy** available at selected Boots stores
08450 70 80 90
**Harrods** 020 7730 1234
**Harvey Nichols** Birmingham 0121 616 6000
**Harvey Nichols** Edinburgh 0131 524 8388,
Leeds 0113 204 8888, London 020 7235 5000,
Manchester 0161 828 8888
**Heidi Klein** 020 7243 5665 www.heidiklein.co.uk
**Helen Kaminski** www.helenkaminski.com,
available at Heidi Klein 020 7243 5665
**Helena Rubenstein** 0800 917 9348
**Helios Homeopathics** 01892 537 254
**Herman Brown's** 0131 228 2589
**Hermès** 020 7499 8856
**Hero** 01223 328 740
**Hobbs** 020 7586 5550
**The Holding Company** www.theholdingcompany.co.uk
**Homebase** www.homebase.co.uk
**Huit** 020 7631 3157
**Human Nature & Nari Sadhuram**
020 7328 5452

**Ikea** www.ikea.co.uk
**Ionithermie** 01753 833 900
**Issa** available at Blossom Mother & Child
020 7589 7500

**The Jacksons** 020 7792 8336
**J. Maskrey** 020 8968 0143 www.jmaskrey.com
**Jan Marini** 01279 814365 www.janmarini.co.uk
**Jane Brown**
020 7229 7999 www.janebrownshoes.co.uk
**Janet Reger**
020 7584 9368 www.janetreger.co.uk
**Jaq** 01225 447 975
**Jason** 020 7435 5911
**Jean Muir** 020 7409 2262 www.jeanmuir.co.uk
**Jean-Paul Mist-On Tan** 0800 783 0056
**Jenny Packham**
available at Harrods 020 7730 1234
**Jerome L'Huillier**
available at Selfridges 0870 837 7377
**Jessica** available at The Natural Nail Company
020 8381 7793
**Jewels** by Jessy www.jewelsbyjessy.com
**Jigsaw** 020 7491 4484
**Jimmy Choo** 020 7584 6111
**J &M Davidson** 020 7313 9532
www.jandmdavidson.com
**Jonathan Aston** 01277 204 744
**John Frieda** 020 7851 9800
**John Galliano**
available at Harrods 020 7730 1234
**John Lewis** 0845 604 9049 www.johnlewis.com
**Johnny Loves Rosie** 020 7247 1496
**John Smedley**
0800 028 6792 www.johnsmedley.com
**Jo Malone** 020 7720 0202
**Joseph** W1 020 7629 6077, SW3 020 7823 9500,
WC2 020 7240 1199, NW8 020 7722 5883,
W11 020 7243 9920, SW19 020 8946 5880,

# S&T'S ADDRESS BOOK

Bluewater 01322 624681,
Manchester 0161 839 0059, Leeds 0113 242 5458
**Joseph M** 01325 489 821
**Juicy Couture & Juicy Jeans**
available at Harvey Nichols 020 7235 5000
**Julie Bloom** 020 7834 4496

**Kalkarrai** 020 7580 9111
**Kangol** 01946 810 312 www.kangol.com
**Karen Millen** 0870 160 031
**Katherine Draisey** 0121 704 2233
**Kérastase** 0800 316 4400
**Kenzo** 020 7493 8448 www.kenzo.fr
**Kimchi** 020 7729 9450
**Kiss Me Mascara** available at Pout
020 7379 0379 www.pout.co.uk
**Knickerbox** www.knickerbox.co.uk
**Koh Samui** 020 7240 4280
**Kookaï** www.kookai.co.uk
**Korner Skincare**
available at Space NK 020 7299 4999
**Korres** 020 7581 6455 www.korres.com

**Lambertson Traux**
available at Harvey Nichols 020 7235 5000
**Lancaster** 0800 379 0688
**Lancôme** www.lancome.co.uk
**La Perla** 020 7291 0930 www.laperla.com
**La Prairie** 01932 827 060
available at House of Fraser 020 7963 2000
**La Senza** www.lasenza.co.uk
**Laundry by Shelli Segal** available at Selfridges
**Laura Mercier** available at Harrods, Harvey
**Nichols** House of Fraser, Liberty and Space NK
020 7299 4999
**Laura Tabor** 07771 660 151
**Le Bourget** available from www.mytights.com
**Lejaby** www.lejaby.com 020 7478 4340
**Liberty** 020 7734 1234
**Lift 6** for salon locations call 020 8731 5678
**The Lift Petite** 01926 438 540
**Linea** 020 7794 1775
**The Linen Press** 01608 650242
**Little London** 01243 539 969
**Liza Bruce** 020 7235 8423
**Liz Lange** available at 9 London and
Serendipity-online.com
**LK Bennett** 020 7290 3560
**Lola Rose** 020 7370 0077 www.lolarose.biz
**Lookfantastic.com** www.lookfantastic.com
**L'Oreal** & L'Oréal Professionnel
www.lorealparis.co.uk
**Louis Vuitton** 020 7399 4050 www.vuitton.com
**Louise Galvin** available at Daniel Galvin Salon
020 7486 8601 and Space NK 020 7299 4999
**Love Kylie** 0870 837 7377
**Lucy's** 01932 847 939
**Luisa Beccaria** available at Selfridges
0870 837 7377 and www.net-a-porter.com
**Lúki** 020 8290 1888
**Lu Lu Anderson** 01373 813 866
**Lulu Guinness** 020 7823 4828
**Lynx** 01423 521404

**MAC** 020 7534 9222
**Madeleine Ann** 0121 704 9454

**Magic Knickers**
020 7371 0276 www.practicalprincess.net
**Maharishi** 0870 888 0910
**Mambo** 020 7384 4403 www.mambo.com.au
**Mandarina Duck**
020 7495 8200 www.mandarinaduck.com
**Mango** 020 7434 3694
**Manolo Blahnik** 020 7352 8622
**Marc Jacobs and Marc by Marc Jacobs**
www.marcjacobs.com
available at Harvey Nichols 020 7235 5000
**Marella** 020 7287 3434
**Maria Grachvogel** 020 7245 9331
**Marie Curie Cancer Care shops**
01793 582 500 www.mariecurie.org.uk/shop
**Marilyn Moore** 020 7727 5577
**Marks & Spencer** 0845 302 1234
**Mark Traynor** available at Screenface
020 7221 8289 www.screenface.com
**Marni** 020 7245 9520
**Mary Cohr** 0808 100 3102
**Matalan** www.matalan.co.uk
**Matches Stores** 020 7221 0255
**Matthew Williamson**
020 7629 6200 www.matthewwilliamson.com
**Maurizio Pecoraro**
available at Matches 020 7221 0255
**Mavala** available at John Lewis 0845 604 9049
**Max Factor** www.maxfactor.co.uk available at
Boots, Superdrug and Pharmacists nationwide.
**Max Mara** 020 7439 2662
**Maybelline** www.maybelline.co.uk
available at pharmacists nationwide
**Megan Park** 020 7739 5828 www.meganpark.com
**Melissa Odabash** available at Heidi Klein
020 7243 5665 www.heidiklein.co.uk
**Me + Ro** www.meandrojewelry.com, available at
**Willma** 020 8960 7296 and Selfridges
**Merola** 020 7351 9338 www.merola.co.uk
**Michael Stars** available from Blossom Mother &
Child 020 7589 7500
**Milli** 0115 950 2882
**Mimi** 020 7349 9699
**Missoni** 020 7352 2400
**Missoni Sunglasses** 020 7730 0202
**Miss Selfridge** 0800 915 9900
**Miss Sixty** 0870 751 6040
**Mister Mascara** 020 7237 1007
**Miu Miu** 020 7409 0900
**Miu Miu Sunglasses** 020 7841 5999
**Mobileffe** available at Chaplins www.chaplins.co.uk
**Moda Rosa** 01962 733 277
**ModelCo** available at Space NK 020 7299 4999
**Molteni & Co** 01484 711 788 www.molteni.it
**Mootich** 020 8960 6066
**Monsoon** 020 7313 3000
**Morgan** 020 7284 7000
**Morgan Clare** 01423 565 709
**Mosaique** 01789 295 820
**Mottoo** 01273 326 633
**Mudd** 01256 844 144
**Muji** 020 7323 2208
**Mulberry** 020 7491 3900
**Myla** 020 7221 9222
**Mytights** www.mytights.com

**Nails Inc.** 020 7499 8333
**Nailtiques** 01543 480 100 www.naturalnail.co.uk

**Nair** available at pharmacies nationwide
**Nari Sadhuram** 020 7328 5452
**NARS** available at Liberty 020 7734 1234 and
Space NK 020 7229 4999
**Natalia** 01803 840 670 www.aboutnatalia.com
**Nawar** 020 8342 8842
**The Natural Shoe Store** 0800 132 194
**Net-a-Porter** www.net-a-porter.com
**Neutrogena** 0845 601 5789 www.neutrogena.com
**New Look** 0500 454 094 www.newlook.co.uk
**Nike** 0800 0561640
**Nine West** 020 7380 3800
**Nirvana Naturals** 01494 880 885
**Nizoral A-D shampoo**
available from pharmacies nationwide
**Nuala by Puma** 01924 425 555 www.puma.com
**NV Perricone** 020 7329 2000

**Oasis** 01865 881 986
**Oenobiol** supplements, available at The Garden
Pharmacy, 020 7836 1007 www.garden.co.uk
**Office** 0845 058 0777
**Office World** www.office-world.co.uk
**Olivia Morris** 020 8962 0353
**Oliver People's**
available at Harvey Nichols 020 7235 5000
**One of A Kind** 020 7792 5284
**Opi** available at Sally Hair & Beauty Supplies
020 7434 0064
**Origins** 0800 731 4039
**The Organic Pharmacy** 020 7351 2232
**Orla Kiely** 020 7585 3322 www.orlakiely.com
**Otazu** 020 7486 1000 www.rodrigootazu.com
**Oxfam** 0845 3000 311

**Parlux Professional Hairdryers** available from
Sally Hair & Beauty Supplies 020 7434 0064
**Paula Dorf** 01444 445 680
**Patrick Cox** 020 7730 8886 www.patrickcox.co.uk
**Paul Smith** 020 7379 7133
**Peacocks** 02920 27 0000
**Pearl Drops** available at pharmacists nationwide
**Peep Show** 020 8505 5111
**Perfectly at Home**
020 7610 8000 www.perfectlyathome.com
**Persol** 020 8955 0770 www.persol.com
**Peter Thomas Roth**
available from Space NK 020 7299 4999
**Philip B** available from Space NK
020 7299 4999 www.spacenk.co.uk
**Philip Kingsley** 020 7629 4004
**Philip Treacy** 020 7824 8787
**Phyto** 020 7620 1771
**Phytomer** 0808 100 2204
**Pilot** 020 7307 3500 www.pilotuk.com
**Pineapple** 020 7379 8090
**Pink Piranha** 020 8800 9258
**Pippa Small** www.pippasmall.com
**Polaris tissue tightening treatment**
available from Dr Jean-Loius Sebagh and good
cosmetic surgeons
**Poliform** 020 7368 7600 www.poliform.it
**Portobello Cashmere Shop** 020 7792 2571
www.portobellocashmere.com
**Portobello Road Market**
London W11, every Saturday

Post Mistress 020 7379 4040
Pout 020 7379 0379 www.pout.co.uk
Powder 020 8347 4100
Prada & Prada Sport 020 7647 5000
Prada Sunglasses 020 8955 0770
Prescriptives 01730 232 566
Pretty Polly 01623 444 299 www.prettypolly.co.uk
Primark 0118 960 6300
Pringle 0800 360 200 www.pringle-clothes.co.uk
Pucci 020 7201 8171
Puma 01924 425 555 www.puma.com
Purves & Purves
020 7580 8223 www.purves.co.uk

Q Clinic 020 7317 1111 www.qclinic.com
Quest available at health food shops
and pharmacies nationwide
Quiggin's Centre
0151 709 2462 www.quiggins.com

Rachel Skinner 020 7209 0066
Rachel Trevor Morgan 020 7899 8927
Ray Ban 020 8955 0770
Red Earth www.redearthbeauty.com,
available at Selfridges 0870 837 7377
Rellik 020 8962 0089
Restylane available from Fiona & Marie
Aesthetics and good aesthetics salons
Revisions 01273 207 728
RéVive 0800 085 2716
Revlon www.revlon.com
Rica Hot Wax treatment
available at Richard Ward and leading beauty salons
Richard Ward Haircare
available at Tesco stores 0800 505 555
Richard Ward Salon 020 7245 6151
Rigby & Peller 01536 764 337
Riemann P20
www.p20.co.uk, available at Asda 0500 100 055
Riley's 01482 868 903
Rimmel www.rimmellondon.com
RMK 020 7259 5669 www.rmkrmk.co.uk
Roaccutane by prescription only
Roberto Cavalli 020 7878 8600
Rodeo Star
available at Harvey Nichols 020 7235 5000
Rodial 020 7565 8307 www.rodial.co.uk
Rokit 020 8801 8600
Ronit Zilkha 020 7330 2888
Royal Elastics
01458 449 349 www.royalelastics.co.uk
Russell & Bromley 020 7629 6903

St. Tropez available at Space NK 020 7299 4999
Sally Hair & Beauty Supplies 020 7434 0064
Salvatore Ferragamo 020 7629 5007
Samsonite available at John Lewis 0845 604 9049
Sand 020 7499 9601
Sara Berman
available at Harrods 020 7730 1234
Sarah Coggles 01904 611 001
SCOPE 0800 800 3333 www.scope.org.uk
Screenface
020 7221 8289 www.screenface.com
Sea Folly 0800 018 0501 www.seafolly.com
Sealkay 020 7436 3037

Selfridges London, Birmingham & Manchester
0870 837 7377 www.selfridges.co.uk
Serendipity-online www.serendipity-online.com
Sergio Rossi
020 7629 5598 www.sergiorossi.com
Sigerson Morrison available at Scorah Patullo
020 7792 0100 and Harvey Nichols 020 7235 5000
Shavata 020 8997 1089
Shelly's 020 7437 0452
Shiseido 020 7630 1515 www.shiseido.com
Shop 020 7437 1259
Shu Uemura
020 7420 7635 www.shuuemura.com
Sign of the Times 020 7589 4774
Simulcium G3
020 7637 0548 www.beautycenter.co.uk
Simultane 01273 818 061
Sisley (beauty) 020 7491 2722
Sixty 6 020 7224 6066
Size? 020 7287 4016
SK-II 0800 072 1771 www.sk2.co.uk
Sloggi
www.sloggi.co.uk, available at www.figleaves.com
Smiths Rosebud Salve 020 7237 1007
Smock 00 353 1613 9000
Sock Shop
0845 130 9595 www.sockshops.co.uk
Solange Azagury Partridge 020 7792 0197
Sotheby's 020 7293 5000
Space NK and Spa.NK
020 7299 4999 www.spacenk.co.uk
Spanx available at www.mytights.com
Speedo 0115 916 7000
Spitfire contact@spitfire-design.com
Sportmax 020 7439 2662
Square 01225 464 997
Square Spots 01446 773 776
Starry Starry Night 0141 337 1837
Stella McCartney 020 7518 3100
Stella McCartney Sunglasses 020 7841 5999
Stephane Kélian 020 7235 9459
Stephane Marais
available at Space NK 020 7299 4999
Stephen Jones 020 7242 0770
Stila 01730 232 566
Strand 01132 438 164
Sublime 020 8510 9960
Sunglasses Hut 020 8955 0770
Swab Plus
020 8554 3335 available at chemists nationwide
Sweaty Betty
0800 169 3889 www.sweatybetty.com
Swiss Army Luggage
available at Selfridges 0870 837 7377
Sybil Stanislaus
(by appointment only) 020 7235 1572

Talika
0870 169 9999
available at Space NK 020 7299 4999
Tamarisk 020 7381 6644
Temperley 020 7229 7957
Tesco 0800 505 555
Textier
available at House of Fraser 0870 160 7258
Thackery's 01604 259 889
Thalgo 020 7512 0872 www.thalgo.com
Tiffany & Co 020 7499 4577

Tisserand 01273 325 666
TRAID 020 8733 2580 www.traid.org.uk
Trish McEvoy
available at Space NK 0870 169 9999
Toller available at Blossom Mother & Child
020 7589 7500
Topshop 0800 731 8284
TSE 020 7629 3286
Tulah available at A la Mode 020 7730 7180
Tulip 01502 725 197
Tumi available at Harvey Nichols 020 7235 5000
Tweezerman 020 7237 1007
Two Stars 01603 764671

Ultimo 0141 427 1010
UltraSwim 01256 844 144

Valentino 020 7235 5855
Valentino Sunglasses 020 7841 5999
Valisere 01536 764 389
Vanilla 01865 552155
Van Peterson 020 7584 1101
Velvet 01707 645 828
Velvet (boutique) 01282 699 797
Versace 020 7355 2700
Vichy 0800 196 6193 www.vichy.com
Victoria Sleeper Vintage Handbags
Stall no. 27, Portobello Antiques Market at
Lonsdale Road, every Saturday 020 7229 5025
Vincent Longo 01252 741 601
Vistoe www.vistoe.com
VV Rouleaux 020 7761 1011

Wade Smith 0151 227 4645
Wallis 0800 915 9901
Wannabee by Patrick Cox
020 7730 8886 www.patrickcox.co.uk
Warehouse 0870 122 8813
Warners 0115 964 6615
Wax A Way available at The Garden Pharmacy,
020 7836 1007 www.garden.co.uk
Weekend Max Mara 020 7439 2662
Weleda 0115 944 8222 www.weleda.co.uk
Wendy Lewis beauty consultant.
For telephone consultations: 00 1 212 861 6148,
for personal consultations in London 020 7201 1699.
www.wlbeauty.com
Whistles 0870 770 4301
Wild Hearts @ Marks and Spencer
0845 302 1234
Willma 020 8960 7296 www.willma.co.uk
Willy's 01392 256 010
Wilson 020 8675 7775
Wolford 020 7499 2549
www.wolfordboutiquelondon.co.uk
Wonderbra 0500 362 430 www.wonderbra.co.uk
Woolworths 01706 862 789

YSL Beauté 01444 255 700
YSL Sunglasses 020 7841 5999
Yves Saint Laurent 020 7235 6706

Zara 020 7534 9500
Ziio available at Fenwick 020 7629 9161

**Susan and Jinny** Editing

**David** Design direction

**Domenic and Natalie** Design

**Robin and Aitken** Photography

**Charlotte** Make-up, and Carol too

**Christiano & Bev** Hair

**Mario** Colour

**Jessica** Everything...

**Zoe & Hayley** Styling

**Michael Foster** Saviour

**Cat** Patience

**Caroline** Organisation

**Antonia** Dealing with clothing chaos

**Oprah** For the opportunity

**Tracy, Vicky, Lindsay** and all at WNTW

**Mr Teoh** For safe deliveries

**Our husbands** For continued support

**Jenny and Kelly** Bringing up babies

**Mrs Seagrove** For Joe and Esme's time off

**and Helle, Theresa, Lynne, Lisa, Kitty, Linda, Penni, Tracy, Sarah and Mickalina,** for teaching us so much more about women.